Ordinary Unhappiness

SQUARE ONE
First Order Questions in the Humanities

Series Editor: **PAUL A. KOTTMAN**

ORDINARY

UNHAPPINESS

The Therapeutic Fiction of David Foster Wallace

Jon Baskin

STANFORD UNIVERSITY PRESS
Stanford, California

STANFORD UNIVERSITY PRESS

Stanford, California

© 2019 by the Board of Trustees of the Leland Stanford Junior University. All rights reserved.

An early version of chap. 4 was originally published as "Untrendy Problems: *The Pale King*'s Philosophical Inspirations," in *Gesturing Toward Reality: David Foster Wallace and Philosophy*, ed. Scott Korb and Robert Bulger, ©2014, Bloomsbury. Reprinted with permission.

This book has been partially underwritten by the Stanford Authors Fund. We are grateful to the Fund for its support of scholarship by first-time authors. For more information, please see www.sup.org/authors/authorsfund/.

Printed in the United States of America on acid-free, archival-quality paper

Library of Congress Cataloging-in-Publication Data

Names: Baskin, Jon, 1980– author.

Title: Ordinary unhappiness : the therapeutic fiction of David Foster Wallace / Jon Baskin.

Other titles: Square one (Series)

Description: Stanford, California : Stanford University Press, 2019. | Series: Square one : first-order questions in the humanities | Includes bibliographical references and index.

Identifiers: LCCN 2018048727 | ISBN 9781503608337 (cloth : alk. paper) | ISBN 9781503609303 (pbk.) | ISBN 9781503609310 (epub)

Subjects: LCSH: Wallace, David Foster—Fictional works. | American fiction—History and criticism. | Literature—Philosophy. | Philosophy in literature.

Classification: LCC PS3573.A425635 Z527 2019 | DDC 813/.54—dc23

LC record available at https://lccn.loc.gov/2018048727

Cover design: Rob Ehle

Cover photograph: Rémi Guillot, Wikimedia Commons

Typeset by Kevin Barrett Kane in 10/14 Minion

Contents

Foreword by PAUL A. KOTTMAN

Before being introduced to Jon Baskin's book on David Foster Wallace, I had never read a word of Wallace's work—in spite of being (I learned from Baskin) a member of the readerly demographic most commonly associated with Wallace. That is, I am identifiably white, male, college-educated, and more or less the right age; I even teach literature and philosophy.

I learned, too, that Wallace's association with such demographics has been taken by some critics as a reason to refuse to read him at all. Other reasons for this refusal include Wallace's personal behavior, especially his treatment of women, his addictions and suicide, sheer human finitude (one only has time to read so many books), and a general skepticism that Wallace's work may not be as good as his advertisers would have us believe.

Learning these facts did not immediately convince me to read Wallace. But the vocal refusal of critics to read Wallace for fear of being duped by marketers put me in mind of what René Girard once called "the Western gullability par excellence": namely, "the obsession with gullability" itself—the shame at being taken by mere representations. "When in doubt," writes Girard, "experts always choose disbelief; this is what makes them experts."[1] Girard was referring to raging, jealous, skeptical Leontes in Shakespeare's *Winter's Tale*. But, of course, such raging skepticism has no demographic limits.

Meanwhile, the refusal to judge Wallace's work because of Wallace himself put me in mind of Theodor Adorno's refusal of jazz—his conclusion that jazz is unfree ("standardizing") because it springs from a fundamentally slavish "psychological" "structure"—"the domesticated body in bondage."[2] I make this analogy not to suggest an equivalence between Wallace and black slaves but to make the point that such criticism does not rest on a judgment about the work itself. Instead, it collapses the space between maker and product—the space of culture. This is to say it expresses not a critical judgment but a prejudice.

Interest in Wallace's work continues to rise. Perhaps this is just a trend, the result of effective marketing. But Baskin sets such worries aside. He is not interested in investigating various causes for our interest in an author's work; and he asks us to shelve *the issue* of whether or not readers personally identify with features of Wallace's life or work. Whether or how to read Wallace is not, finally, a question about "Wallace," Baskin suggests; it is a question about us. More to the point, Baskin suggests that Wallace's work knows this—that it invites us to bring the world of which Wallace writes to a fuller awareness and knowledge of itself. With Robert Pippin and Stanley Cavell as his companions, Baskin shows how this kind of self-knowledge is both psychological and sociohistorically indexed. He draws our attention to the way that Wallace's fiction is itself a world—one that challenges the reader to face it without asking *whether* it is true or actual or moral but what it could mean to see that it is true and actual, and with what moral implications.

Baskin calls Wallace's fiction "therapeutic," and although Kant is not discussed in these pages, I was continually put in mind of Kant's view that there are things that we cannot know, scientifically, but that we also cannot doubt. For example, I cannot "know" that you are in pain—I cannot know the "pain itself" (whatever that may mean)—but I am missing something crucial if I doubt you when you tell me that you are hurting. There are moral (and aesthetic) domains, in which our relationship to things we need to understand are not knowledge-based relations but rather meaning-based relations, so to speak. Moreover, an important step in the direction of addressing moral-aesthetic claims is made when we see that our reliance on certain ways of thinking, certain forms of knowing, can impede this step. Because Baskin convinced me that Wallace understood this, and that his fiction shows us the pervasiveness of a damaging reliance on certain forms of thinking, he convinced me to devote attention to reading Wallace's work.

Baskin asks what the value of his kind of literary criticism *is*—what *good* it is. And he offers a number of thoughtful responses to this first-order question. But one answer must be that his critical judgment might bring new readers to Wallace and thereby bring Wallace into the orbit of broadly shared concerns—deepening and refining our understanding not of Wallace but of those concerns themselves.

Abbreviations

Ordinary Unhappiness

Introduction

Habits of Mind

THE VERY FIRST philosophical challenge to the arts remains the most daunting. Considering the role of art in their ideal city, Socrates and his interlocutors in Plato's *Republic* settle on two options: censorship or exile. Poets and painters can either abide by the "models" philosophers have established for educating good citizens—limiting themselves to "hymns to the gods of the city" and the like—or they can take their leave.[1]

The argument against artists unfolds in two stages. In books 2 and 3 Socrates deals with art predominantly in terms of the kind of activity it promotes—for example, deception and imitation—and when he returns to it in book 10, he begins by summarizing and adding to his earlier account of the inherent dangers of poetic imagery. But later in the same book, he clarifies that his argument against artists, or "image makers," does not rest primarily on a suspicion of their tools. Philosophers, as Socrates himself has demonstrated in his allegory of the cave, also use poetic imagery. What distinguishes the image maker is that she does not know what the images she uses are for. When Socrates says that poets are imitators in the "highest possible degree," he means not that they are the most skilled at making images but rather that, absent any higher criteria of value, their use of images can answer only to the low logic of the marketplace—that is, to what is popular or pleasing to their audience.² That is why those "praisers of Homer who say that this poet educated Greece" are mistaken: Homer could not have educated Greece because Homer's poetry prioritizes "pleasure and pain" over "that argument which in each instance is best in the opinion of the community."³

Having completed his case against poets, Socrates pauses to consider what a shame it will be to live without them. He finds great pleasure in tragic theater, and he reflects that he will regret having to give up that pleasure for the sake of justice. With this in mind he asks defenders of art for an "apology" that would convince him to allow Homer and the tragedians back into his ideal city.

Beginning with Aristotle's idea of catharsis—according to which citizens purged their unproductive emotions at the theater so that they could become more virtuous and rational citizens outside of it—many such apologies have been attempted over the years, by philosophers, by literary critics, and sometimes by philosophically inclined artists like Tolstoy. Yet contemporary philosophers are even more dismissive than Plato was of the idea that the imaginative arts can contribute to philosophy. Plato had at least acknowledged the need to argue, repeatedly and at length, for the banishment of the artists. Since Descartes, the main tradition of Western philosophy—with the notable exceptions of Nietzsche and Heidegger, who both sought to overturn Plato's hierarchy and thus put the artists in charge—has trusted that poetry can either be safely ignored or presented as an ornamental accompaniment to an education in theoretical reason. In *The Cognitive Value of Philosophical Fiction* the philosopher Jukka Mikkonen lays out the various positions taken by today's professional philosophers in the "perennial debate" about whether literary works "may provide knowledge of a significant kind." According to Mikkonen, the majority of philosophers today believe either that fiction does not provide significant philosophical knowledge or that it is capable of doing so only by offering philosophical propositions—as in a Dostoyevsky or Thomas Mann novel, where characters who may be presumed to speak for the author advance explicitly theoretical views. In other words, most of today's philosophers believe fiction can contribute to philosophy only by becoming it.

Mikkonen does mention a small group of philosophers—Martha Nussbaum, Stanley Cavell, Robert Pippin, and Cora Diamond among them—who have maintained that literature can provide philosophical knowledge nonpropositionally by, as Mikkonen puts it, elevating our ethical understanding, educating our emotions, stimulating our imagination, or calling our moral views into question.[4] This group falls mostly into a semicontiguous progression of moral philosophers—stretching back to Ludwig Wittgenstein and his English-language translator G. E. M. Anscombe—that is considered heterodox, if not entirely alien, to the broader Anglo-American tradition. One of their distinguishing features is that they turn to literature not to find case studies that confirm their philosophical theses but rather to challenge what they take to be the dominant mode of *doing* philosophy. This means the mode of philosophy that takes its cues from the sciences rather than the arts. When, famously, at the end of his book *The Claim of Reason*, Stanley Cavell asks whether philosophy, if it were to accept poets back into its vision of the just city, could "still know itself," the question implies that mainstream philosophy's self-identification has become inextricable from its refusal of the literary.[5]

The present study is not an apology for literature so much as an attempt to help philosophy know itself in the fiction of David Foster Wallace—a writer who in both his biography and his fiction exhibited an unusual blend of philosophical and literary motivations. The point of this attempt is twofold. First, and mainly, I hope it will contribute to a better understanding of Wallace's fiction. Currently, the consensus among commentators is that Wallace was an uncommonly "philosophical" fiction writer, but there is no consensus regarding what it means to say this. Aside from certain aspects of his biography,[6] the agreement is based mostly on the observation that Wallace's books are dotted with allusions to figures in the Western philosophical tradition, that his characters occasionally engage in philosophical discussions a la *The Brothers Karamazov*, and that reading some philosophy is helpful for fully appreciating what is going on in certain of his passages. These are all ways in which Wallace's fiction engages with philosophical concepts or language. The argument of this book, however, will be that Wallace's fiction is not just sporadically or instrumentally philosophical but that his project as a whole is structured by an encounter among habits of thought he considers to emanate from different modes or ways of doing philosophy.

A second claim of the book will be that the "therapeutic"—which is the name I give, following Wittgenstein and Cavell, to the mode of philosophy Wallace privileges in his fiction—offers a fertile ground on which philosophy and literature can, so to speak, do something together. I do not see this potential cooperation as a matter of merely academic interest. When Cavell questioned whether philosophy's exile of the poets had come at too high a cost, he was suggesting that the Platonic separation of philosophy from literature, reinstituted in the Enlightenment under the aegis of Cartesian rationalism, had limited our ability to address the particularity of our modern social and moral experience. He was writing, primarily, with his fellow professional philosophers in mind. But the plays of Shakespeare and Beckett that Cavell himself would analyze, the novels of Proust and James whose philosophical thinking has been presented by Robert Pippin, and the fiction I discuss in this book, by David Foster Wallace, give ample indication of why the estrangement of art from philosophy is a problem for more than *philosophers*.

Often, Wallace correlates the concrete suffering of his characters with their bewitchment by a picture that features, among other things, a conflation of thinking in general with the form of skeptical, analytical thinking that modern philosophy valorizes above all others, including and especially the form of nonthinking it associates with art. For Wallace, the separation of philosophy from literature—and the crude dichotomies often correlated with that separation: mind/body, theoretical/practical, intellectual/emotional—are *both a cause and a symptom* of a "dis-ease," as he calls it in *Infinite Jest*, at the heart of modern and postmodern self-consciousness. Bringing philosophy and literature together becomes the precondition for even being able to *see*—much less to address or "treat"—the many symptoms of this dis-ease in our everyday lives and in ourselves.

DIFFERENT THERAPIES

The word *therapy* comes from the Latin *therapia*, and from the Greek *therapeia*, meaning "curing, healing, service done to the sick." It can be proper to speak of almost any medicine or course of treatment for a health problem as a "therapy," and health professionals will often speak of "gene therapy," "hormone therapy," and so forth, in just this way. In common speech, however, we tend to use the word *therapy*, especially in reference to the kind of "talking cure" that has been popularized since Freud: this is usually what we mean when we ask someone if they have "been to therapy." The relevant difference, for our purposes, has to do with the patient's level of participation in, and awareness of, the treatment. When the therapy is purely physiological, the patient will not be able to give any nonscientific account of how it has improved her health. The ideal of Freudian therapy—to make the unconscious conscious—however, links a cessation of suffering to the achievement of self-understanding, which is what makes it so potentially congenial to philosophy. It is also why Freudian therapy originally and for many of its inheritors still focuses predominantly on etiology and diagnosis, under the presumption that these are the fastest routes to self-knowledge and, thereby, health.

The later Freud would, however, deemphasize the importance of diagnosis and etiology in favor of procedures by which the psychoanalyst, especially through the process of transference, could compel analysands to recognize how they were applying (or "projecting") habitual or inherited frames of understanding onto a new situation. No matter how well analysands understood the distant causes of their current suffering, the thought went, it was only through being able to recognize its operation *in situ* that they could begin to free themselves from it. The later Freud thus prefigures in various ways Wittgenstein's methodological—or "metaphilosophical" in Paul Horwich's formulation[7]—commitment to philosophy being therapeutic rather than theoretical. This commitment meant seeing philosophy less as a method for exposing logical fallacies than for catching philosophers "in the act" of reflexively applying a frame—for instance, a "metaphysical frame" or a "positivistic frame."[8] What was required to correct the problem the philosopher was working on was not a better theory, or a more salient understanding of the phenomenon in question, but rather the therapeutic insight that came from seeing how the problem emerged out of the frame. The key passage for understanding Wittgenstein's notion of philosophy as therapy comes in *Philosophical Investigations*:

> The real discovery is the one that makes me capable of stopping doing philosophy when I want to.—The one that gives philosophy peace, so that it is no longer tormented by questions which bring *itself* in question.—Instead, we now demonstrate a method, by examples; and the series of examples can be broken off.—Problems are solved (difficulties eliminated), not a *single* problem.
>
> There is not *a* philosophical method, though there are indeed methods, like different therapies.[9]

Commentators who have addressed the philosophical content of Wallace's fiction have acknowledged and occasionally focused on Wallace's explicit references to Wittgensteinian arguments and themes, such as solipsism, or meaning-as-use—the latter of which is the subject of a monologue in Wallace's first novel, *The Broom of the System*. I intend to build on this commentary but also to make the further argument that Wallace's fiction as a whole can be viewed as a continuation of Wittgenstein's philosophical project by other means. In calling Wallace's mature fiction therapeutic, I mean to imply that it is best looked at as a "series of examples," intended to therapeutically expose and treat not only a set of problems but also a point of view, or what Wittgenstein would have called a "picture."

ARGUING DIFFERENTLY

What was that picture? To answer this question, we must first ask another. Who are Wallace's readers? This question suggests itself to many critics, even if they have no investment in the idea of Wallace as a philosophical therapist. Mark McGurl has argued that any description of Wallace's fiction is "insufficient without some account also of his readership, that social body to which his works are directed and in which they seek completion."[10] Such a statement reflects the fact that Wallace's readers have often betrayed an unusually intimate relationship with his writing. Visible manifestations of this relationship have included the 2009 "Infinite Summer" project, which brought together "bibliophiles from around the world" to read and discuss Wallace's one-thousand-page novel in seventy-five-page weekly chunks,[11] as well as the 2015 film *The End of the Tour*, which chronicles four days in Wallace's life at the end of his *Infinite Jest* book tour. The film elicited deeply personal reactions among both Wallace's supporters and his critics.[12]

The passion and pathos of responses to Wallace's work testify to the fact that the fiction itself is "dialogical," not just in the Bakhtinian sense that it gives credence to contradictory voices or viewpoints but also in the Platonic sense, revived by Wittgenstein, of a philosophical writing that attempts to simulate a dialogue between the author and his audience. (Wallace himself frequently referred to his fiction as a conversation.)

So far, accounts of Wallace's readership have most often been given in terms of demographics. McGurl, for instance, hazards that Wallace's readers are "largely young, educated, middle-class white people, mostly but not exclusively men."[13] Such a description—endorsed by Wallace himself in his conversations with journalist David Lipsky[14]—might be verified or refuted by sales figures, work partially undertaken by the critic Ed Finn in an illuminating essay that examines Amazon.com data and readers' comments about Wallace's books.[15] Or it might be compared with the anecdotal experience of feminist commentators like Amy Hungerford and Deirdre Coyle, both of whom have written about being besieged by highly educated white men who insist that they accept Wallace as a "genius."[16] It could also be justified by looking at the statistical breakdown of those who have chosen to write articles or books about Wallace—most of whom are white and male, like me.

My approach to the question of Wallace's audience, however, will begin from a different starting point. Since I'm attempting to understand the thinking or method behind Wallace's fiction, I'm more interested in what it is about the stories themselves that makes such demographic descriptions seem natural than I am in whether they are accurate. For to answer *that* question means turning away from demographic data and anecdotes and toward the books themselves—that is, to the kinds of characters that appear in Wallace's fiction and to the sorts of problems that are dealt with in them.

Luckily, an outline of these problems can be sketched on the basis of the very first short story Wallace ever published. Written while he was still in college, "The Planet Trillaphon as It Stands in Relation to the Bad Thing" (PT) is told from the point of view of a teenager on antidepressants. Trillaphon is the name the boy gives to the planet on which he feels the antidepressants have stranded him (the specific drug he's been prescribed is called Tofranil, but to himself he refers to it as Trillaphon, based on the "trilly and electrical" [PT 18] feeling he has when he's on it), where he is doing "somewhat better" than he was doing back "on Earth" (PT 5). The story begins, however, by describing why the boy had had to leave Earth in the first place, on the principle that "if someone tells you about a trip he's taken, you expect at least some explanation of why he left on the trip in the first place" (PT 5). He had had to leave Earth because of what he calls the "Bad Thing": clinical depression. The majority of the story is taken up with his description of what it was like to live with that depression.

Two related features of this description are significant for appreciating the kind of reader Wallace seems to have thought he was addressing. The first is that the narrator of the story presents himself as having been in pain. The second is that the narrator indexes this pain, not to any external stimulus or event—a childhood trauma, poor treatment by friends or parents, late capitalism, and so forth—but to his *form of thinking*. In fact, the narrator locates the source of his problems *entirely* in his way of talking to himself. In language that could equally be applied to Hal Incandenza in *Infinite Jest* (see Chapter 2), or to the "depressed person" in *Brief Interviews with Hideous Men* (see Chapter 3), the narrator describes his pre-antidepressant self as a "troubled little soldier who could withstand neither the substance nor the implications of the noise produced by the inside of his own head" (PT 9). The way to combat the Bad Thing, he goes on to say, is "clearly to think differently, to reason and argue with yourself, just to change the way you're perceiving and sensing and processing stuff" (PT 12).

Wallace addresses a readership he presumes to be in pain and one whose pain is connected to, and possibly a function of, a certain way of thinking. These points are not seriously contested in Wallace commentary. But so far, we have only outlined the mental predicament of Wallace's audience; we still need to bring out the set of assumptions or "connections"—as Wittgenstein would have called them—that Wallace suggests condition their picture of the world. Not every feature of that picture is evident in "Planet Trillaphon." But what I take to be a structuring feature of that picture is indicated in the boy's conflation of "thinking differently" with the ability to "reason and argue with yourself." What the boy assumes will "change the way" he perceives the world and quiet the "noise" in his head is a sound argument. This is what thinking differently amounts to for him.

That this assumption is not just a function of the boy's personality or of his immediate cultural or demographic environment, but is rooted in a *philosophical* confusion, is indicated when the boy describes how he feels when he is depressed, namely, "like Descartes at the start of his second thing" (PT 10). The "second thing" refers to the "Second Meditation," which begins with Descartes's admission that "yesterday's meditation has thrown me into such doubts that I can no longer ignore them, yet I fail to see how they are to be resolved. It is as if I had suddenly fallen into a deep whirlpool; I am so tossed about that I can neither touch bottom with my foot, nor swim to the top."[17]

The whirlpool metaphor gives a clue to why the comparison might have recommended itself to Wallace—he has just compared the feeling of depression to being "under a body of water that has no surface" (PT 10)—but it hardly exhausts its implications. One could say that it is in Descartes's second thing that the tenor of modern philosophy is established. Having, the previous day, been thrown into doubt—having thrown himself into it—about such fundamental questions as whether or not he is awake and exists, the philosophical investigator decides that he will "stay on the course" he has undertaken until he knows "something certain, or, if nothing else, until I at least know for certain that nothing is certain." By the end of the meditation, he has convinced himself that there is one certain thing: his thinking. This means that he is "precisely nothing but a thinking thing; that is, a mind, or intellect, or understanding, or reason."[18]

My point is not that Descartes must have been depressed when he came to that conclusion but that depression, for the narrator of Wallace's story, is related to a Cartesian approach to problem solving. In situating what ails his characters in such a way, Wallace suggests that, whatever their problems, they cannot *merely* be attributed to exposure to pervasive popular media or to the addictive distractions of consumer capitalism—or even to the morally noncommittal rhetoric of the popular advanced art and theory that Wallace believed had come to dominate his era intellectually. All of these cultural phenomena play prominent roles in the mature Wallace's fiction and at different times contribute to or exacerbate the dis-ease of his characters. One of the truly philosophical things about Wallace as a thinker, though, is that he considers culture *as a whole* to be oriented by certain ideals or pictures. Whatever habits of mind have come to feel natural to his characters will also have influenced the institutions that shaped those characters. In its focus on the internal argument the protagonist has with himself, "Planet Trillaphon" reveals what Wallace believes to be most fundamental: as if in an endless feedback loop, the Cartesian approach both informs and is informed by all the usual postmodern suspects.[19]

Art in general, and Wallace in particular, has at times been associated with a challenge to Descartes's seemingly limiting conclusion that we are "thinking things."[20] This is not, however, the assumption that Wallace contests in his fiction; he does not, that is, propose that faith, or affect, or blind obedience to something bigger than ourselves represent ways of proceeding that are superior to "thinking." What he does contest is Descartes's assumption that the same *kind of thinking* that threw the boy into a whirlpool of doubt will prove capable of rescuing him from it. For Descartes, the way to assuage doubt is to arrive at the knowledge of "something certain." One achieves this knowledge by reasoning one's way to the right theory, which means a theory that corresponds to a "true" state of affairs. And this reasoning involves—a subsidiary point but an important one for Wallace, as it was for Wittgenstein—the theoretical redefinition of certain words and concepts, such as "seeing" or "thinking," for otherwise the investigator may be "deceived by the ways in which people commonly speak."[21]

The guiding "picture" of serious thinking according to Descartes begins with the questioning of common language and common sense—that we are awake, that we exist, that we know what a word like *awake* means—and proceeds, via what W. V. Quine called "semantic ascent,"[22] to establish certainty about common usage or common sense where beforehand there had been either doubt, ambiguity, or an ungrounded *illusion* of certainty. The technique is modeled on scientific practice and mathematical proof. Its criteria of success are (a) the invulnerability of its premises to logical counterargument and (b) a conclusion that allows us to replace confusion or error about some phenomena with certainty, even if that certainty consists in our knowledge of the impossibility of certainty—an outcome for which Descartes allows. To put it explicitly (as Stanley Cavell often did), this tradition of thinking assumes that there are only two conclusions, once it has undertaken the investigation of a given phenomenon: certainty or skepticism.

Wallace is hardly the first to question this either/or aspect of Descartes's procedure, which has been subject to deep challenges by Nietzsche, Heidegger, and Wittgenstein, among others. What distinguishes Wallace's engagement is his identification of Descartes's approach with what has become a habitual way of thinking about the self—and not just among philosophers. This way of thinking about the self may, Wallace concedes, have its uses, but it offers no comfort to a person in pain. Often, it ushers them ever deeper into the regressive spiral of doubt that has given rise to the pain in the first place.

The beginnings of Wallace's response to the problem can be glimpsed with reference to the fact that, in "Planet Trillaphon," it is not a better theory—or, as the boy might put it, "*arguing* differently"—that changes the boy's experience of the world. Within the story there is only one thing that makes the boy feel "somewhat better": the antidepressant Tofranil. It is not a complete solution. The boy misses several things about being back "on Earth," feels distant from other people and himself, and worries that the Bad Thing will eventually reappear on his new planet. At the same time, the way he describes his new state of being demonstrates something about what Wallace believed was involved in "thinking differently." On Planet Trillaphon the boy sees things differently than he did on Earth. But this is not because he has come up with a new *argument*. In fact, he cannot say *why* he no longer feels the force of the Bad Thing, now that he is on that planet. He simply is not in its grip anymore. The story may be received as an exposition on Wittgenstein's pronouncement from the *Tractatus*: "The world of the happy man is a different world from that of the unhappy man."[23]

But I choose to focus on this early short story because it offers an unusually transparent view of the picture that Wallace wants to treat, not because it provides a model for how he later endeavors to treat it. From a therapeutic perspective, "Planet Trillaphon" plants the seeds of its own self-criticism when the boy, having just delved into the details of his previous depression, confesses that "even thinking about it a little bit and being introspective and all that, I can feel [the Bad Thing] reaching out for me" (PT 12–13). We can take this to reflect Wallace's own caution about the pitfalls, and the seductiveness, of Cartesian-style introspection. The story itself, however, recruits our sympathy for a character unable to do much more than expose us to his pain and to report that a drug has made him feel "somewhat better" about it. As with much other fiction about depression, it thus risks romanticizing its subject's solipsism and sadness, precisely the kind of thing that some critics have warned is characteristic of Wallace's fiction as a whole. A second danger is that it can encourage the "frankly idealistic" assumption that Wallace associates, in his 1992 essay on television, with "early postmodern irony," namely, that "etiology and diagnosis pointed toward cure, that a revelation of imprisonment led to freedom."[24] (This assumption goes back at least to Freud, if not to Descartes.)

Insofar as Wallace presumes that fiction can and should do more than simply describe and diagnose pain—that it should try and "treat" it—his story hints at a need for a new form of storytelling. To view his mature fiction as a "series of examples" is to view it as a series of treatments for what Wallace takes to be the various forms of cultural confusion and despair that are related to the picture I have begun to sketch. These treatments differ from Tofranil in many respects, but they resemble the role the drug plays in Wallace's story insofar as they endeavor to change our perspective in ways not reducible to arming us with new or better arguments. If they do not always show us what the world looks like to the happy man, they at least demonstrate that the world of the unhappy man is not the only world.[25]

One thing that follows from calling Wallace's therapies philosophical, as opposed to physiological, is that we should be able, unlike the boy, to offer some kind of account of how they work. But what kind of account would this be? Based on "Planet Trillaphon," all we know is that these treatments will *not* depend on Cartesian-style argumentation and explanation. This is the sense in which I will make a case for how the specific form of Wallace's fiction is related to his ambition as a philosophical therapist, with his "patient" being both the individual reader and the form of life that has produced that reader's habits of mind. Central to that case will be the distinction between a theoretical approach to such habits of mind and a therapeutic one.

◆ ◆ ◆

Because this book is an argument for the virtues of an approach to imaginative literature, in addition to being a study of a fiction writer, my first chapter examines what I call philosophically therapeutic literary criticism. This will be done in part through a discussion of my own experience studying "literature and philosophy," as well as an examination of how therapeutic philosophy and literary criticism are blended in the works of Iris Murdoch, Robert Pippin, and Stanley Cavell, among others. Chapters 2 through 4 present readings of three of Wallace's mature works of fiction—*Infinite Jest* (1996), *Brief Interviews with Hideous Men* (1999), and *The Pale King* (2011)—all in view of the "different therapies" that organize the relationship between their content and their form. In my chapter on *Infinite Jest* I focus on the Wittgensteinian challenge (especially evident in the AA sections) that is posed to the Cartesian picture (especially evident in the opening scene) of what Pippin has called "modern and postmodern self-consciousness";[26] in the chapter on *Brief Interviews* I home in on Wallace's treatment of a particular way of speaking about other people, which has consequences for the relationships we form both in everyday social life and through literary fiction. In the chapter on *The Pale King* I will emphasize what distinguishes Wallace's literary-philosophical therapy from the more conventional forms of therapy with which many of his own characters experiment throughout his fiction. These readings are the interpretive heart of the book, on which my strategy of interpretation will rise or fall. In my conclusion I return to the question of what it means to conceive of Wallace as a philosophical artist—and ponder whether we might do better to think of him as an artistic philosopher.

WALLACE STUDIES

As I will argue in Chapter 1, the therapeutic critic often begins by looking at how an artwork has previously been perceived or interpreted: there, the critic finds a record of how a work has been taken in the past to either confirm or challenge the philosophical "picture" of its readers. Although "Wallace Studies" is still a relatively young field, there is a significant body of criticism relating to Wallace's fiction, particularly to his mid-career opus, *Infinite Jest*. In the ensuing chapters I will address some of that criticism as it pertains to specific novels and stories. Here, though, I want to emphasize what I see as a unifying tendency among Wallace's early academic commentators: the inclination to treat his fiction as if it were enacting precisely the kind of certainty vs. skepticism mode of theoretical argumentation that I am suggesting it endeavors to undermine.

Early academic responses to Wallace's fiction almost invariably concluded that it could be utilized to illustrate or advance arguments about subjectivity, language, or media from the era of Big Theory. In *Consider David Foster Wallace* (2010), the earliest collection of academic essays on Wallace, Wallace's fiction is associated with theoretical constructions previously worked out by Ricoeur, Baudrillard, Jameson, Rorty, and Derrida, among others. An initial problem with such an approach is that Wallace's fiction was often in dialogue with the ideas and rhetoric of such thinkers and therefore could not be reduced to a demonstration of them. A larger problem is that critics approaching Wallace's fiction in this way tended to give the impression that he was engaged primarily in a theoretical debate—regarding the impossibility of the "unitary self" (Clare Hayes-Brady), or the death of the autonomous subject (Mary K. Holland; N. Katharine Hayles), or the "cultural expansion" of consumerism in postmodern society (Connie Luther)—whereas in my view his fiction is engineered to challenge our attraction to not just one specific theoretical argument or another but to the theoretical mode of seeing and thinking as a whole.[27] More sophisticated criticism of Wallace's fiction appeared in the ensuing years, and frequently it focused on a more plausible evaluation of his project with regard to postmodern and other theory. Although the second wave of Wallace critics sometimes associated Wallace's ideas with that of prominent literary theorists—for instance, Adam Kelly sees his approach to communication as Derridean, while Lee Konstantinou calls his conception of institutions "vaguely Focauldian"—usually to misleading effect, they have also recognized his animus against the most familiar manifestations of high-postmodernist theory. The more recent group of critics have often gone even further, concluding that Wallace considers our contemporary intellect to be so hopelessly corrupted by media, or culture, that he appeals instead to his readers to become "post-ironic believers" (Konstantinou), to invest their "Blind Faith" in him as an author (Kelly), to reconnect with their feelings (Timothy Aubry), to take a "leap of faith" (Zadie Smith), or to give over their agency to the care of institutions (Mark McGurl).[28]

As an example of this second wave of Wallace commentary, I want to pause briefly on Kelly's "David Foster Wallace and the New Sincerity in American Fiction," which has been called "the best work" to come out of the Consider David Foster Wallace conference that gave rise to the collection.[29] I choose it in part because it represents one of the most sophisticated engagements with the philosophical intent of Wallace's fiction and because, in focusing on sincerity, it addresses a topic that was clearly important both to Wallace and to his critics. Virtually since Wallace's name began to enter the public consciousness, it has been thought that he was advancing some novel theory of literary communication and especially of literary sincerity. Yet in attempting to describe that theory, his critics have often fallen into the very Cartesian trap that Wallace was trying to chart a course out of. This is to say that they seem ineluctably pulled toward a frame for their investigations of sincerity in Wallace's fiction according to which Wallace *either* advances a new theory of sincerity *or* he attempts to demonstrate that sincerity is simply an inappropriate object for rational consideration.

Kelly's essay represents the most sophisticated and perceptive entry into the literature on Wallace and sincerity, connecting Wallace's self-conscious rhetoric about sincerity and intentionality with Derrida's use of a certain "way of writing" to undermine the "metaphysical assumptions" of his audience.[30] I am sympathetic, especially, to Kelly's claim that for Wallace "true sincerity" and intention could never be guaranteed theoretically; indeed, Kelly shows how Wallace's familiarity with the "use" of sincerity in modern advertising and art ("sincerity with an ulterior motive," as Wallace called it)[31] had made him especially sensitive to sincerity's unverifiability in any given circumstance. At the same time, Kelly's conflation of Wallace's and Derrida's approach to sincerity commits him to an all-or-nothing path with regard to our ability to communicate sincerity. It is as if, having concluded that sincerity cannot be proven theoretically, Kelly is *forced* to the conclusion that it must be illusory, something we only imagine we know anything about.

The two steps Kelly takes down this path are instructive. He begins by establishing that Wallace shares Derrida's impression that it is impossible, in practice, to ever determine for certain whether "any single event of giving or receiving is the genuine article or not." Having established this, Kelly next suggests that Wallace must also agree with Derrida that there is therefore "no way to present sincerity positively in cognitive terms."[32] Were it not for those somewhat ambiguous final two words ("cognitive terms"), the statement that there is *no* way to present sincerity positively might immediately strike us as an extreme jump from the claim that no single act of communication can *prove* itself to be sincere. Yet the qualification has dropped out by the time Kelly suggests, a few pages later, that "in Wallace's fiction the guarantee of the writer's intentions cannot finally lie in representation—sincerity is rather the kind of secret that must always break with representation."[33]

The position is calculated to repel what are taken to be two mistaken views about intentionality and sincerity in literature. One is the naive view that the author's intentions are obviously present on the surface of a given text; the other is that true sincerity can be ascertained if one looks deeply enough into the text, using the right theoretical tools. Neither of these conclusions is wholly satisfactory: the first appears to be innocent of the problem—as if a writer's intentions were always perfectly transparent—while the second misrecognizes the problem as what Cavell would call a problem of knowledge.[34] Kelly is right to reject both positions as insufficient, but, from what I am arguing is the Wittgenstein-Wallace perspective, his rejection of the second position turns out to be incomplete, since it accepts that position's framing of sincerity and intentionality as concepts with abstract theoretical content that, in ideal (say nontextual) conditions, it would be possible for us to achieve certainty about. Since it is not possible for literature to provide those conditions, Kelly, drawing on Derrida, claims that literary intentionality and sincerity must be "secrets," lying "beyond representation" and capable of being accessed *only* through an act on the reader's part of "trust and Blind Faith."[35]

Cavell has shown why Wittgenstein would, when a discussion seemed to be speeding along such a track, appeal to our "ordinary" use of language. Wittgenstein's point was not that ordinary language is always superior to theoretical language—for some purposes, theoretical or technical language is clearly superior—but that such an appeal can sometimes bring us to confront "the illusions produced by our employing words in the absence of (any) language game which provides their comprehensive employment (cf. §96)."[36] The illusion produced by Kelly's discussion of "sincerity"—which he conducts through Lionel Trilling with the philosophical tradition—is that *sincerity* can mean anything at all once it is abstracted from its role in a specific act of communication. Part of the task of Wallace's fiction is to remind his reader of the contexts that give concepts like intentionality and sincerity their urgency in the first place. How do I deduce what you intend from what you say? *It depends.* If we are face-to-face, I might look you in your eyes, interpret your body language, or consider—if I have known you for a while—how far your words are supported by your past behavior. Art may not allow for *those* kinds of considerations, but that does not mean we are cast with it into an abyss of guesswork and omens. If I have read enough, I will get a feel for when a writer means what she says. I might find that her writing helps or hurts me—that it knows or is ignorant of my true needs. Or I may not be able to shake the sense that I am being merely flattered—that not enough is being required of me or that the author is simply "showing off." There are *countless* ways for me to judge, based on the words I hear or read, the sincerity of their author.[37] Because Kelly accepts the premise that sincerity and intentionality can be interrogated as theoretical abstractions, he is led to posit that, if they are not completely transparent to our analytical reason, then the reader must only be able to access them via some non-rational process like intuition or faith. But it is precisely this premise, or "conjuring trick," that Wittgenstein teaches us to take note of. The dichotomy only appears attractive once we make the problem seem theoretical as opposed to practical. In the case of literary intentionality this move has been habitual for academic critics since at least the days of Wimsatt and Beardsley's "intentional fallacy." Once the theoretical problem appears, it appears to be insoluble.[38]

For Wallace, the tendency to make personal and interpersonal problems into theoretical problems—and then to try and solve them via abstract argument—was itself connected to the despair or "lostness" that he observed in his friends and contemporaries. He did not mean only to question the "metaphysical assumptions" of his readers but also, and more distinctively, to address their habit of *making their problems look metaphysical.* "The first step is the one that altogether escapes notice," wrote Wittgenstein. "We talk of processes and states and leave their nature undecided. Sometime perhaps we shall know more about them—we think. But that is just what commits us to a particular way of looking at the matter."[39] It is this first step—often in an argument his characters are having with themselves—that Wallace's therapy is intended to expose the importance of. For once the problem has been detached, so to speak, from its foundations,[40] no amount of "arguing with ourselves" will close the gap.

The therapeutic task, then, is not to find some "secret" solution that will close that gap but to bring the concepts in question *back*, as Wittgenstein famously put it, "from their metaphysical to their everyday use." I read this as Wittgenstein's gloss on Freud's famous explanation of his psychotherapeutic method, which I have used for the title of this book. Many of his patients, Freud said at the end of *Studies in Hysteria*, wondered how he could help them when so many of their problems were grounded in their "circumstances and fate." But the goal was not to solve all of the problems of life—only the ones they had made for themselves. "You will see for yourself that much has been gained," Freud told his patients, "if we succeed in turning your hysterical misery into ordinary unhappiness."[41]

◆ ◆ ◆

I began this book at a different time than I am finishing it. Of course, this is true of all books in a trivial sense. The gap is significant in this case because, in the years since I began writing, there has been a series of notable revelations about David Foster Wallace's biography and character. Before he hanged himself at his California home in 2008, Wallace spoke occasionally—and wrote (in his fiction) voluminously—about his battles with depression, narcissism, and drug and alcohol addiction. In D. T. Max's 2012 biography, *Every Love Story Is a Ghost Story*, we learned that, in addition, Wallace was frequently a bad friend and a self-involved lover, who treated women poorly and sometimes worse than that. In a series of tweets earlier this year, Wallace's one-time partner, the writer Mary Karr, alleged that he had threatened or physically assaulted her on more than one occasion.

In a few recent articles such revelations have been combined with anecdotal details about the kind of people who read Wallace's books, often with the implication that echoes of Wallace's intellectualized misogyny can be found in many of his most avid readers. For instance, in a widely circulated April 2017 post for *Electric Literature*, entitled "Men Recommend David Foster Wallace to Me," Deirdre Coyle bemoaned the regularity with which Wallace's short story collection *Brief Interviews with Hideous Men* had been recommended to her by chauvinistic male classmates and partners.[42]

Commentators have, sometimes implicitly and sometimes explicitly, marshaled the evidence of Wallace's biography and reception against his fiction. Although she does end up reading *Brief Interviews* for the purposes of the article, Coyle seems to agree with the literary critic Amy Hungerford's contention, in her essay "On Not Reading

DFW"—published in part in the *Chronicle of Higher Education* and later collected in her 2016 book, *Making Literature Now*—that the revelations from Wallace's biography should make us question whether it is worthwhile to read his fiction at all. Putting the reports from Max's book together with a piece of dialogue from one of Wallace's early novellas, interpreted as signaling Wallace's belief that a writer should set out to "fuck the reader," Hungerford contends that "the link between Wallace's art and his relationships with the people he slept with bears considering."[43] After considering it, she decides that what she knows about both Wallace's life and his art justify a decision to abjure finding out more.

In addition to Wallace's misogyny Hungerford raises his struggles with addiction—not to mention his admiration for the Mel Gibson film *Braveheart*—as further reasons for skepticism about the moral value of his writing. She and Coyle both stop short, however, of acknowledging the most brutal evidence against the wisdom of Wallace's art, perhaps because it had already been indicated years earlier by the novelist Jonathan Franzen. In his 2012 essay for the *New Yorker*, entitled "Farther Away," Franzen, allegedly a close personal friend of Wallace's, interspersed details of his trip to the island of Masafuera to scatter his friend's ashes with a reflection on the "infantile rage and displaced homicidal impulses" that he says led to Wallace's suicide.[44] Franzen's discussion of Wallace, unlike Hungerford's or Coyle's, is complicated by his admiration for Wallace as a prose stylist; nevertheless, Franzen goes even further than Hungerford or Coyle in interpreting Wallace's life against his art. For Franzen, Wallace's suicide should serve as the capstone to a cautionary tale for readers tempted to follow him onto the "island of solitude," where he was a lifelong prisoner.

Details about an author's life or reception are not always essential to considerations of their work. How we view Wallace's life in relation to his art, however, is complicated precisely because he conceived of his role as an artist in therapeutic terms: he might have objected to Mark McGurl's characterization of him as a "popular moral educator,"[45] but it is undeniable that he conceived of the benefit of his fiction as lying in something other than mere pleasure, entertainment, or beauty. It is against the background of Wallace's own contention that his fiction could address the collective "lostness" of his readership, as well as the testimony of some of his readers that they have been helped or uplifted by Wallace's novels, that Hungerford expresses her desire to pierce "the glow of Saint Dave" (147), that Coyle wishes to deflate Wallace's reputation among her smug male friends, and that Franzen endeavors to combat the "adulatory public narratives" (43) that he says grew up around Wallace after his death. Such narratives, Hungerford, Coyle, and Franzen imply, must be based predominantly on privilege or hype—Hungerford infers that *Infinite Jest*'s success was the product mainly of clever marketing—or the inability of impressionable young men to tell the difference between wisdom and charismatic nonsense. Moreover, they seem to ask, somewhat as Plato does about Homer in the *Republic*,[46] if Wallace was such a wise writer, why aren't his readers more virtuous?

The lines of argument pursued by Hungerford, Coyle, and Franzen represent challenges, but also opportunities, for a critic wishing to make a case for the *value* of Wallace's project. How can we know that Wallace's fiction about misogyny is not, as Hungerford says, just "more misogyny"? How can we know that Wallace's writing about narcissism and addiction does not lead, as Franzen indicates, to more narcissism and more addiction? How can we be sure that Wallace's fiction does not lead to suicide? The truth is that we cannot *know*. Yet while such questions may seem melodramatic, or embarrassing, they are only extreme versions of the questions we ask ourselves whenever we decide to invest time and energy in a work of fiction, especially a "difficult" one that takes weeks of our lives to complete. As Hungerford points out: There are so many books, so why spend our precious hours reading these?

We cannot and should not forget what we know about an artist's biography when we are interpreting her work. This knowledge is part of what we bring to the work—no less relevant or deniable than the knowledge we bring about our own lives or the culture and society that we and the author share. But just as we cannot deny the influence of what we know, so we ought to remain open to what might be in a work that challenges what we think we know. Hungerford, at one point, admits that Wallace seems to have "sensed where an interesting question lay," then asserts that there is no evidence to suggest that he "did anything more than put us in sight of a good question." I would not be as quick as Hungerford to trivialize the achievement of putting us "in sight" of a good question, but this book will take up her challenge: what "more" does Wallace's fiction offer us? Why *would* I recommend Wallace's fiction to anyone, including myself? Thankfully, for those of us who believe there is a great deal more in Wallace's novels and stories than Hungerford suspects, such questions all point in one direction: back to the books.

1

Narrative Morality

On Philosophically
Therapeutic Criticism

An outstanding question is then: What sends us back to a piece or a
passage?—as though it is not finished with us.

— Stanley Cavell, "The Avoidance of Love"

EARLY IN MY ACADEMIC CAREER, I began to probe the intersection between literature and philosophy. I was motivated by
something like the following thought: the best literature is not just
"literary"; it involves ideas, and the best philosophy is not just logical; it employs literary tropes and often a creative use of language
or rhetoric. As a critic or scholar, I thought, I could help show how
reading philosophy as literature and literature as philosophy would
illuminate the meanings of both. And beneath this thought lay another: that when properly understood, the greatest literature and the
most convincing philosophy were part of a complementary intellectual and ethical project.

Aside from some colleagues there were many professional academics, in both English and philosophy departments, already working at
this intersection. But there seemed to be little agreement among those

academics about what it meant to study literature philosophically or vice versa. The field, such as it was, was held together less by a well understood mission than by a set of complaints against those who misunderstood the mission. On the one side, said the philosophers, there were literary scholars, who peppered their criticism with shallow bursts of "theory," often ignorant of the context or complexity of the ideas they claimed were supported or challenged by imaginative texts. On the other side, said professors of literature, were the philosophers, who threatened to reduce fictional narratives to a series of case studies for illustrating their argumentative theses.

Neither side of this (exaggerated) dichotomy are static or monolithic, of course, and during my years in graduate school thinkers from both proposed ways in which their discipline—literary studies or philosophy—might benefit from a fuller interaction with its counterpart. In English departments a group of critics including Stephen Best, Sharon Marcus, Bruno Latour, Franco Moretti, Lisa Ruddick, Elizabeth S. Anker, and Rita Felski, sometimes described as initiating a turn to "postcritque," have called for a "rethinking" of literary studies, particularly in regard to the field's adoption of critical methods from the era of Big Theory, such as the "hermeneutics of suspicion."[1] Not all of these critics agree on what should replace critique; some—Moretti, most conspicuously—have turned to the sciences or the "digital humanities" in hopes of promoting a more objective form of reading; others, like Marcus and Best, have suggested "surface reading" as a corrective to forms of interpretation that emphasize texts as bearing hidden or "symptomatic" meanings in their depths.[2] Not all of these techniques, as Merve Emre has pointed out, are as "non-normative" or "radical" as they pretend to be,[3] and some simply extend the project to "rationalize literary studies on various grounds"—often by attempting to make it more "scientific"—that Timothy Aubry describes as having been the animating motive of English departments for the past seventy years.[4]

Some of these critics, however, in their search for tools capable of reconfiguring the theory-centric paradigms of reading in their discipline, have looked not to the theoretical sciences but to ordinary language philosophy. Revealingly, the first essay in Anker and Felski's *Critique and Postcritique* is by Toril Moi, who turns, for a corrective to the methodology of critique and theory, to philosophical therapy. In the essay Moi, who has written a book about ordinary language philosophy and literary studies,[5] proposes a model for criticism that takes its cues from the philosophically therapeutic procedures of Wittgenstein and Cavell. Referring to Wittgenstein's notion that "a description is the therapy we need to see clearly," she argues that the literary critic's work is not to critique or "demystify" the text but to describe it, as Wittgenstein might say, perspicuously.[6] As she demonstrates vividly in her essay "Describing My Struggle," about the series of novels by the Norwegian novelist Karl Ove Knausgaard, this involves not just describing the interrelations between various elements within the text but also bringing out what the work has to do with *us*, its readers.[7]

As should already be evident, I agree with Moi that Wittgenstein and Cavell provide promising resources for those working at the intersection of philosophy and literature. In turning to Wittgenstein and Cavell, however, it is important to note that Moi does not just avail herself of the resources of the discipline known as "philosophy"; she draws from a specific tradition of philosophical thinking that is characterized and even defined by its marginality. Just as those challenging the usefulness of critique and symptomatic reading remain in the minority in today's English departments, so those working in the tradition of Wittgenstein and Cavell are in the minority in today's philosophy departments; they are even in the minority of the minority within those departments who pay attention to literature.

As I mentioned in my introduction, the present study aims to help philosophy "know itself" in David Foster Wallace's fiction. But the focus of this chapter will be somewhat narrower and more self-regarding. How, I want to ask, can someone who wants to write *about* literature philosophically go about promoting the kind of (self-)knowledge that critics like Cavell and Moi believe can be found in it? For it is not obvious, according to many of the claims that this camp of philosophers makes for artworks, why an interpreter would be necessary at all. If I am right that David Foster Wallace's fiction is a form of philosophical therapy, what is left for me as a critic to do besides tell you to read it?

With that question in mind, after a brief history of what is sometimes known as the "nonpropositional" philosophical approach to literature,

I will focus on two philosophers who have significantly influenced my own way of reading literature: Robert Pippin and Stanley Cavell. Looked at together, they provide one roadmap for how a philosophical critic can bring out the therapeutic thinking in a work of literature even, and perhaps especially, when that thinking is aimed at challenging prevailing assumptions about what it means to think philosophically.

ENDLESS TASKS

When Cavell raised the question of whether philosophy's Platonic "exile" of the poets had come at too high a cost, he was drawing on a line of thinking that might be said to begin with G. E. M. Anscombe's landmark 1958 essay, "Modern Moral Philosophy."[8] Anscombe, who is also known as the foremost English translator of Wittgenstein, attacked what she called "consequentialism" as an umbrella term for the theories put forward by the previous two centuries of significant moral philosophers. Anscombe did not mention literature at all, but she did draw attention to both the difficulty and the limitations of judging moral action according to abstract rules or by reference to their potential consequences. The problem with the approach of previous moral philosophers was plain, she reflected, once one acknowledged that, in most actual as opposed to theoretical cases the rightness or wrongness of an action was contextual—and thus could only be really *seen* by "giving examples" (188).

Philosophers have always used examples *from* literature to support their arguments, but Anscombe's observation inspired some to go further. Literature is not only a place where one can find convenient case studies; it is where one can observe, as one cannot in mainstream philosophy, the workings and development of the moral imagination. In *The Sovereignty of Good* (1970) the philosopher and novelist Iris Murdoch chooses a narrative she says should be familiar from "innumerable novels" to illustrate Anscombe's point about the narrowness of the frame used by conventional moral philosophy. The narrative involves a mother, "M," who initially feels hostility toward the woman "D," whom her son has married, considering her to be "lacking in dignity and refinement." Despite the hostility she feels toward her, M always treats D with propriety and kindness. Over the years, however, she begins to come to a different conclusion inwardly about D; having "looked again," she realizes that D is "not vulgar but refreshingly simple, not undignified but spontaneous." This change is not expressed in M's external behavior toward D or in any discernible action she takes—yet, Murdoch insists, we want to describe such a change in perspective as *moral*:

> What M is *ex hypothesi* attempting to do is not just to see D accurately but to see her justly or lovingly. Notice the rather different image of freedom which this at once suggests. Freedom is not the sudden jumping of the isolated will in and out of an impersonal logical complex, it is a function of the progressive effort to see a particular object clearly. M's activity is essentially something progressive, something infinitely perfectible. So far from claiming for it a sort of infallibility, this new picture has built in the notion of a necessary fallibility. M is engaged in an endless task.[9]

The story does not prove a point or rule about morality. Rather, it shows us, via a certain kind of description, the shape that a moral development might take. Just as important, the described action takes place in time—that is, in narrative—and would be incomprehensible apart from it. M does not simply make a decision one day about D, applying whatever criteria or rules she has deliberated on; rather, she finds that, paying attention to D over time, in a "progressive effort to see" her clearly, her opinion of her gradually evolves, eventually to the point where she is able to see her "justly or lovingly."

For Murdoch, to admit that such an "endless (inner) task" belongs within the realm of moral philosophy amounts to nothing less than the "liberation of morality, and of philosophy as a study of human nature, from the domination of science: or rather from the domination of inexact ideas of science which haunt philosophers and other thinkers."[10] Here can be glimpsed the continuity of Murdoch's and Anscombe's thought with Wittgenstein's, particularly in the portion of his *Philosophical Investigations* that is devoted to debunking the predominant—and largely scientistic—notion among the philosophers of his time of "ideal analysis." What can also be seen is the pressure in both cases for philosophy to become more literary. This pressure does not come about because literature offers examples to complicate or confirm philosophy's theories but for the linked reasons that literature (1) gives us narratives that show how moral actions take place in time and space and therefore (2) holds the power to cure or correct traditional moral philosophy's (over)reliance on static rules or theories. This would seem to be one of the (endless?) tasks of the "philosophy of psychology" that Anscombe calls for.

The aforementioned section in *Philosophical Investigations* (roughly §81–§133) concludes with Wittgenstein's insistence that "there is not *a* philosophical method, though there are indeed methods, like different therapies" (§133). Like Murdoch, Cavell and Pippin seem to have been influenced by the way that section recasts philosophy's work as one of "rearrangement" and "description," as opposed to one of "explanation."[11] The shift in method comes with, or is motivated by, a shift in focus. Philosophical problems are not "empirical problems," Wittgenstein says, the key to which would be something "abstruse" or "hidden." Rather, "the aspects of things that are most important for us are hidden because of their simplicity and familiarity."[12] The philosopher's job is not to make our language more precise, or to "resolve a contradiction by means of a mathematical or logico-mathematical discovery," but to "assemble reminders for a particular purpose."[13] What we need to be reminded of is the "frame" or "foundation" of our inquiry, the very thing that, because it seems so natural to us, is hardest to catch hold of. Cavell sometimes describes this concept of philosophy as one in which the goal is to bring "the world of a particular culture to consciousness of itself."[14]

Both Pippin and Cavell approach imaginative literature—or some imaginative literature—as having the potential to bring its readers to consciousness about relevant features of their historical or philosophical pictures of the world. More to the point, these works expose what might be taken by such a reader as simply being "given" *as* a picture— and therefore something that might be relinquished—or chosen—as opposed to being merely reproduced or capitulated to. Although there is nothing wrong with their doing so, readers need not "identify" with the characters in a book in order for this process to occur; it would be better to say that, if the critic's description is convincing enough, readers will be unable to escape recognizing the image of themselves in the book. To call that recognition philosophical is simply to refer back to the notion—in embracing it, Wittgenstein was picking up on a thread that goes back to Plato—of philosophy as a self-critical activity, whose aim is to produce a kind of (self-)knowledge, unlikely to be arrived at through either unexamined practical experience or "pure" logical analysis. Indeed, as I will argue in Chapter 4, Wallace's own therapy was aimed in part at the prevailing modern prejudice that logic, or theory, represents the "ideal" route to knowledge in every circumstance.

Before moving on to their specific readings of literature, I want to mention a significant difference in emphasis between Pippin and Cavell. Both seem to take up certain aspects of Wittgenstein's notion of philosophy as therapy. But Wittgenstein is not the only or even the most significant influence on their approach to literature: Pippin's approach is influenced deeply by Hegel; Cavell's is informed at various critical points by Freud. The result is that, while both speak of literature's ability to bring readers to *consciousness* about their condition, the word *consciousness* carries a different emphasis depending on who uses it. In Cavell's case the concept has psychoanalytic implications, whereas for Pippin it often has predominantly historical or political ones. This is not to deny what both philosophers insist on—that there can be no clear dividing line between collective history and individual psychology.

PHILOSOPHICAL LITERARY CRITICISM: ROBERT PIPPIN

It might seem paradoxical to call Pippin's approach to literature "therapeutic" at all, given that one of the targets of his criticism is what he calls "psychological" readings of characters in the novels he chooses to discuss. If characters like Strether or Marcher in Henry James's fiction, or the narrator, Marcel, in Proust's *Remembrance of Things Past*, are often considered of interest primarily for their psychology, Pippin characteristically wants to show their psychology to be a symptom of something more general and objective. For Hegel, art was one of the organs through which a society could reflect on—by making explicit to itself—its form of life, which meant not only its habits of thought or speech but also the institutional structures and power relations that continuously shaped those habits. Much of Pippin's philosophical criticism of literature is devoted to making explicit how novelists like James and Proust can help us recognize configurations of thought that are less eccentric than common, less a function of individual history than of "the situation of modernity itself."[15] One of his recurrent points is that exclusively psychological readings of individual action can itself become a sociohistorical habit, so seemingly "natural" to us that we cease to see it as a choice.

That so much of our social and communal life has become so fine-grained and circumstantial that it is difficult, from any amount of distance, to see as anything other than the result of arbitrary pathology is in large part why Pippin believes the novel "might be the great modern philosophical form."[16] He means that novels can show in a manner that philosophy cannot—or has not been inclined to—how ordinary people struggle to be recognized as moral agents and to do justice to the claims of others in the everyday social world. As a novelist, Henry James is bound to treat moral life less as a matter of abstract rules than "as a matter of mores, and that means as a matter of essentially social and historically specific practices, institutions, and largely implicit rules and expectations." And this is particularly appropriate for documenting "one of the most confusing and complex periods" of historical transition—the modern period, which we still inhabit.[17] If we might think, from the overhead view of ideal analysis, that the new historical world James depicts leaves no choice but moral skepticism—a conclusion reached by many modern philosophers and some of its novelists—James's novels do not so much argue for a different conclusion as they show how we "go on" confronting moral claims in our everyday lives, despite and in some cases because of the uncertainty caused by the breakdown of shared criteria for moral judgment.

In attempting to bring out this feature of James's fiction, Pippin's philosophical criticism of literature tilts against two tempting readings of modernist novels. At one end of the spectrum, there is the psychological reading I have just described, whereby characters like Marcel (*In Search of Lost Time*) or Strether (*The Ambassadors*) or John Marcher ("The Beast in the Jungle") are personally eccentric or psychologically "interesting" in ways that are said to be reflective of their author's own eccentric proclivities or that have to do with their veiled homosexuality, their artistic sensibility, their abnormal passivity, and so on.[18] At the other end of the spectrum are critics who perceive such characters and situations as expressive of timeless, existential conditions—say, the condition of human aloneness (in Marcher's case) or our inability to lay hold of our immediate experiences (in Marcel's). For Pippin, both the psychological and the existential or metaphysical readings leave out precisely what should make the thinking in such novels relevant to a contemporary reader: they miss what it is that is being brought to consciousness by the work in question. For this has directly to do with the historical situation—the "modern moral life"—of which the novels offer both a reflection and a diagnosis. The trouble Marcel has interpreting his experience is not best received as a metaphysical statement about the human condition; it is rather "historically indexed, tied to the sort of world where sexual identities can seem to change instantaneously, information circulates rapidly and often without context, and moral hierarchies crumble and are rebuilt unpredictably."[19] Likewise, Marcher's difficulties with time and memory, far from simply mimicking some of the well-known personality traits of his author, should suggest to the contemporary reader "larger problems with historical time and this historical time in particular."[20]

Such readings are philosophically therapeutic insofar as they offer not a psychological interpretation of the novels but a re-presentation of the novel's thinking that allows its readers to see their own psychology—as reflected in the habits of thought of James's or Proust's characters—in a new light. To say that James tells us about modern moral life is to claim for his fiction the kind of moral-philosophical role that Hegel prescribed for art, which could externalize features of historical life that might otherwise remain merely sensuous or implicit and therefore insensible to reason or evaluation.[21] For Pippin, what modernist novels illustrate (in the Anscombean sense) much better than does the kind of philosophy published in academic journals is why and how, in our historical moment, "the achievement of free subjectivity requires a certain sort of social relation among subjects, and that this relation of mutuality and reciprocity is highly sensitive to social arrangements or work and power and gender relations."[22] What James's novels describe, perhaps most conspicuously through the example of Strether in *The Ambassadors*, is a journey from a merely superficial or constrained sense of oneself as a free agent to a more durable form of freedom that rests in part on a "greater capacity . . . to take account of others better" and therefore to better account for oneself.[23]

As with the example I took from Murdoch above, it can be seen why this kind of moral realization would be difficult to explore *outside* of an artistic narrative. On the one hand, the characters in the novels of Proust or James—and Pippin would later apply a similar framework to the films of Tourneur and Welles—have the (very modern) desire to be independent, free agents, yet in their capacity as fictional characters within a social world they are surrounded by reminders of their "profound dependence on others," or they are forced to come to terms with "how terribly *limited* explanations that focus on the moral psychology of individuals turn out to be . . . given how unstable, provisional, and often self-deceived are their claims for self-knowledge."[24]

That the anxiety caused by the conflict between what these characters want and what they encounter in their social world—between the desire for independence or autonomy and the fact of dependency or entanglement—has itself become a background feature of life in modernity is precisely why it is so important to attend to cultural forms capable of making that conflict explicit, thereby allowing us to negotiate it at least somewhat consciously. For the alternatives, as the novels Pippin treats make clear, involve either the assertion of a false and unsustainable freedom for the individual or a capitulation to the various forms of moral skepticism and nihilism that our culture makes available to us every day.

PHILOSOPHICAL LITERARY CRITICISM: STANLEY CAVELL

Pippin's philosophical reading of literature only partially answers the question with which I began this chapter: if works of art themselves are philosophically therapeutic, then what work is there for the *critic* to do? Stanley Cavell addresses this question more directly in his essay on *King Lear*, "The Avoidance of Love," where he speculates about something he calls "philosophical [art] criticism." If such a thing existed, he suggests, its objective would be to bring "the world of a particular work . . . to consciousness of itself."[25]

This way of addressing it can, however, seem obscure in several ways, not least because a work of art, properly speaking, does not possess a "consciousness." I think Cavell is trying to draw our attention to the fact that a particular work of art, like a particular culture, *is* a world and that, as in any world, certain aspects will be seen at first glance (and maybe even at thousandth glance) more easily than others. But what is not easily seen is not necessarily something that is hidden deep in the work, awaiting the right scholar to track down the relevant allusion or the right theorist to fit it into its proper place. Rather, just as a whole culture may be unaware of what is most familiar or natural to it, so what has not been seen by a particular work's audience is often hidden in plain view; it is something whose "meaning has been missed only because it was so utterly bare."[26] This does not mean Cavell is an early adopter of "surface reading"; to the extent that what he identifies is a problem of critical method, the method itself is imagined as the symptom of a much deeper blindness or repression. Psychoanalytically speaking, the best literary works will be characterized in part by their bearing a message for their reader that is "unspeakable"; that this message is hiding in plain sight does not make it any easier to decipher.

This ascribes an unusual double function to the philosophically therapeutic critic. On the one hand, the critic is faced with the burden that every critic faces: making the reader see what the critic has recognized in the work. On the other hand, the critic will have to account for how something that is already in plain view could have been so easily missed in the past. If criticism can be described as the history of a culture's attempts to read and contend with a work of art, then the therapeutic critic will have to analyze this history to see what might have motivated the culture to miss what is now revealed as the work's "obvious" meaning. That is why, just as Wittgenstein's "therapies" often begin by imagining the genesis of a particular philosophical blindness, so Cavell begins his essays on literature by engaging with the interpretations of canonical critics. The point is not primarily to argue with their conclusions but to hold them up as testaments to "the difficulty of seeing the obvious"[27]—or whatever is obvious in that particular work of art. This is also why what the therapeutic critic has to say to us, if we accept it, must eventually seem obvious, as if we had known it—but not been able to describe it to ourselves—all along.[28]

The most striking example of this method in Cavell's criticism comes during his discussion of Lear's motivation in the opening scene of *King Lear*. Despite the long and distinguished history of Shakespeare criticism, Cavell argues that there has never been a satisfying interpretation, or description, of the king's seemingly erratic behavior, including his harsh treatment of his most faithful daughter, Cordelia. The problem with the customary explanations for Lear's behavior—that Lear is ignorant or senile, that Shakespeare could think of no other way to get his drama going—Cavell suggests, is not only that they are incomplete or inconsistent with what else we know of Lear's character (or Shakespeare's talent) but also that they fail to account for the scene's power over its audience—that is, for the audience's willingness to *accept* what happens in it.

Cavell's "discovery" is that Lear's behavior in the opening scene, if we can only see it clearly—as opposed to theoretically or from the vantage point of how it all comes out—is "far from incomprehensible. . . . It is, in fact, quite ordinary." An aging king accustomed to being flattered for his power, Lear is doing something common enough for a patriarch: he is trying to "brib[e] love out of his children." And it goes like it often does, except with a twist at the end. Two of Lear's daughters "accept the bribe, and despise him for it; the third shrinks from the attempt, as from a violation." So Lear punishes Cordelia not because he is mad, or stupid, or because he misreads her refusal to flatter him as expressing a lack of love but because he "*knows* she is offering the real thing"—that is, a love that scorns flattery, and is thus "putting a claim upon him he cannot face." She threatens both to expose his plan and to "expose the necessity for that plan—[Lear's] terror of being loved, of needing love."[29]

This claim of Cavell's, if we are inclined to accept it, is one that we as readers almost cannot face, since it will have, as Cavell says in another context, "the effect of showing us that it is *we* who had been willfully uncomprehending, misleading ourselves in demanding further, or other, meaning where the meaning was nearest."[30] Why "willfully" uncomprehending? Because the critic here seems to provide the most *obvious* account of Lear's motivation—yet we had failed to see it. It is not difficult to grasp this motivation intellectually (it is devastatingly easy to grasp), and once we have been told about it, we can hardly deny that there is evidence for it in the play. So we can only conclude that we have failed to see it because we did not wish to see it. Literary criticism is often perceived as a process of looking under the surface of the text, but therapeutic criticism—in both Cavell's and Pippin's hands—is concerned with what has kept us from seeing what is right on the text's surface. It seeks to expose not something hidden in the work of art but something we have hidden from ourselves. That is why one may not only be surprised by its critical discoveries but also ashamed by them.

In his essay on Beckett's *Endgame*, entitled "Ending the Waiting Game," Cavell also begins by pointing out the "quite ordinary" aspects of what might look at first to be exotic or mysterious. Critics, he observes, have emphasized the "extraordinary" nature of the happenings in Beckett's drama, but the four gnomic figures are "simply a family"; they "bicker and reminisce . . . and comfort one another as best they can."[31] Their dialogue, flat and alien as it looks, is no more extraordinary than our own; the difficulty for the reader is not so much to interpret the sentences in the play as it is to contend with what they simply say. This is not the same as insisting that the play is "realistic"; indeed, Cavell argues that *Endgame* exposes the comforting fraudulence of much of what we call realism (that may be one of the games it is meant to be the end of). What Cavell exposes is how the work implicates its audience in precisely the moments where it looks strangest or most distant. The critical task becomes not to find out how the behavior of such figures and words can be made consistent, or logical, but to make it clear what they have to do with *us*.

Lest this be mistaken for the command to "identify" with characters, I think it is actually something like the opposite. We cannot "see ourselves in [Beckett's] characters," Cavell writes, "because they are no more characters than cubist portraits are particular people. They have the abstraction, and the intimacy, of figures and words and objects in a dream."[32] And as figures in a dream they do not "*invite* us" to take them personally—nor does Cavell. That we *do* take them personally is the data he begins with, as if—to extend the analogy—he were a psychoanalyst approaching a patient's dream. The patient is the whole culture that produces and receives such a work of art. That words and figures "*can* mean in these combinations," that *these* four figures can be a family, is presented by Cavell not as something the viewer should or could ask herself to imagine but as a fact she will have to confront if she wants to explain the play's meaning to herself at all.[33]

In Cavell's and Pippin's essays on literature the artwork does not then "model" a way of dealing with ethical challenges; still less does it offer universalizable ethical guidance or contain propositional knowledge. Rather, the artwork itself *constitutes* an ethical and philosophical challenge. The critic's role is to help the reader face it.

◆ ◆ ◆

Toril Moi, in her essay "Nothing Is Hidden," identifies this difference between the kind of criticism practiced by many in her academic discipline and philosophically therapeutic criticism: whereas the suspicious literary theorist presumes that the "text is hiding something from us," she writes, the Cavell/Wittgenstein critic presumes that "the problem is *in me, in us*."[34] In other words, the artwork's value comes from showing readers something about themselves. But this assessment, with which I agree, still leaves open the question with which we started: if the artwork itself does the work of therapeutic enlightenment, what is left for the critic to do?

Moi attributes her answer to Cavell, who says that "a certain sense of the question 'why this?' is essential to criticism."[35] This is to say that philosophically therapeutic criticism does amount to a recommendation, perhaps to a wider audience than might normally be attracted to it, to attend to *this* artwork rather than some other. But that is not the only work of the therapeutic critic. Such a critic is also motivated by the sense that, even for those who do attend to the artwork, it will be easy for them to avoid or misrecognize its therapy. The therapeutic critic must therefore account not only for what she sees in the work but also for why previous readers and critics have *missed* it. This is why, as Cavell put it, the therapeutic critic is also always a cultural critic. She negotiates between the culture's fantasy of the artwork, preserved in the critical conversation about it, and the artwork itself, which holds within it the prospect of what Murdoch called "the freedom from fantasy." (As if to state the therapeutic benefit of such freedom, Wittgenstein called this freedom "peace.")[36]

Of course, it is an assumption of the philosophically therapeutic critic that works of literature and works of philosophy are or can be, as I mentioned at the beginning of this chapter, engaged in a complementary project. Indeed, the conjoining of the work of *Philosophical Investigations* with the work of an ostensibly avant-garde drama like *Endgame* threatens to go further, blurring the line that even many working at this intersection seem invested in maintaining between art and philosophy. Moi has written that we "do not wonder about the relationship between philosophy and literature because we have trouble telling them apart."[37] Granted that this is rarely the starting point for inquiries into that relationship; however, the questioning of our conventional categorizations can seem unavoidable once that inquiry gets going. Once we have begun to see something we recognize as philosophical knowledge in a theater production, how can we *know* that *Philosophical Investigations* is a work of philosophy at all or that *Endgame* is not one?

Cavell has suggested that one of the reasons professional philosophers have been hesitant to take seriously Wittgenstein's comparison of philosophy to therapy is that it leads so seamlessly to the conclusion that the artist is either equal to, or a competitor of, the philosopher.[38] Plato did consider this possibility, and the culmination of his consideration was that the artists should be censored or banished. Today's philosophers maintain rather different assumptions, and I have heard some object that, when Cavell compares Wittgenstein and Beckett, for instance, he is conflating two distinct and possibly incommensurate kinds of problems—the problems dealt with by the artist (practical or psychological problems, or the problems of life) and the problems dealt with by the philosopher (the problems of logic or reason). The philosopher who stumbled into a blind alley in logic is not, this objector will say, really comparable to the kind of person who populates Beckett's plays—or, as we will see, Wallace's fiction—for this is a figure in intense emotional or psychological distress.

It would not be fatal for the Cavell-Pippin approach to literature to admit that there are philosophical problems that are disconnected from the problems of life; these, we might say, are not the problems that have interested modern artists, nor do they speak to the potential confluences of literature and philosophy. At the same time, I hope I can go some way toward showing, or bringing attention to how artists like Wallace show, the problems of philosophy and of practical life to be interrelated, not only in their content but also in their structure. Cavell sees this as a primary lesson of Wittgenstein's later philosophy, and I believe it is just as much a lesson of Wallace's mature fiction.

Wittgenstein and Wallace both begin with a sense that their readers are in severe distress. The former says his readers are "tormented" by "deep disquietudes," the latter that they are "depressed," "sad," or "lost." And both portray this distress as simultaneously philosophical *and* practical or personal. Again and again in Wittgenstein we think we are treading safely in a region of philosophical logic, and suddenly we are plunged into the most concrete kind of concern ("How am I filled with pity *for this man*?").[39] Over and over in Wallace we think we are dealing with a concretely emotional or practical distress, when the problem is suddenly revealed to be one of philosophical method ("[I was] going around and around inside the problem instead of really looking at the problem.")[40]

If Cavell wondered whether philosophy could still "know itself" if it became literature, Wallace's fiction helps us see how the failure to do so is not merely an abstract or an academic problem; it is indicative of our form of life and of that life's characteristic disappointments and disconnections. Insofar as Wallace's fiction is calculated to help us see the *connection* between psychological suffering and our habits of thought, it not only demonstrates the potential interrelation of literature and philosophy; it is about some of the consequences, both philosophical and practical, of their estrangement.

2

Playing Games

Infinite Jest as
Philosophical Therapy

He could just hunker down in the space between each heartbeat and make each heartbeat a wall and live in here. Not let his head look over. What's unendurable is what his own head could make of it all. What his head could report to him, looking over and ahead and reporting. But he could choose not to listen.

—David Foster Wallace, *Infinite Jest*

PUBLISHED IN 1996, David Foster Wallace's *Infinite Jest* became a best seller despite running more than one thousand pages, including more than two hundred pages of small-print endnotes, and earning a reputation as an "exemplar for difficulty in contemporary fiction."[1] Like Thomas Pynchon's *Gravity's Rainbow* or Don DeLillo's *Underworld*, the book contains a vast panoply of characters and situations, with the connections between them clarifying gradually (but in some cases never completely) as the novel unfolds. Because of its surface resemblance to those earlier landmarks—in addition to the conspiracy-laden plot, there are convoluted sentences, digressions on technology and media, reproductions of emails and fake interviews—

it was read by early reviewers as the next big postmodern novel or, in the (in)famous words of the *New York Times*'s Michiko Kakutani, as a pretentious "word machine," which left its reader "suspended in mid-air and reeling from the random muchness of detail and incident."[2] Other professional reviewers linked *Infinite Jest* with the works of contemporaries like William Vollmann, Rick Moody, and Bret Easton Ellis, a group perceived as carrying on the project of the canonical postmodernists. In an influential review for the *New Republic*, James Wood grouped Wallace with Don DeLillo and Zadie Smith as the vanguard of an offshoot of postmodern orthodoxy, which he dubbed "hysterical realism" (it was not meant as a compliment).[3]

Later scholars and literary critics have recognized that *Infinite Jest* can be read, at least in part, as a response to what Wallace considered the excesses of his postmodern forebears. Both Marshall Boswell and Stephen Burn, in lengthy works on Wallace, have connected the novel with the search for a literary "third way" that moves beyond what had become a set of stultifying quarrels between modernism and postmodernism, although without entirely disavowing the formal techniques of either.[4] Lee Konstantinou has situated Wallace as a "post-ironist," attempting through his fiction to create "believers" in a secular age,[5] and Adam Kelly has focused on Wallace's commitment to the artistic and moral value of sincerity, which cuts against early characterizations of his project as pretentious, cold, or excessively abstract.[6] Similarly, Timothy Aubry has read the novel as directed therapeutically against what Wallace perceives as his self-consciously intellectual readership's "inability to feel" deep and authentic emotion.[7]

Helpful as these corrections are to the early view of Wallace as a grateful inheritor of the postmodernist tradition, they fail to do justice to Wallace's full animus against postmodern thinking. It is symptomatic of even the most insightful Wallace criticism that it often culminates by ascribing to him a theoretical position—for instance, against the "illusion of autonomy" (N. Katherine Hayles)[8] or for the Derridean questioning of "certain metaphysical assumptions" (Kelly)—in familiar postmodern debates. Even Konstantinou, who positions Wallace against "historical postmodernism," ends up reading his project as "vaguely Foucauldian."[9] Such criticism misses not only the target of Wallace's project but, so to speak, its depth. To bring "the world" of *Infinite Jest* to consciousness of itself is to bring to consciousness how strongly we as readers may be implicated in the problems it attempts to address. This is, in the first place, to see postmodernism not as a set of distinct arguments or artworks, which we may already consider antiquated or academic, but rather as a symptom of a modern philosophical "picture" that still determines both what we take to be our most serious problems and how we go about trying to solve them.

The novel's real "difficulty" lies not in its long sentences, its digressions, or its allusions to poststructuralist critics (Wallace's readers were ready for those challenges) but rather in what it endeavors to get its reader to see. The demographic of those likely to read a novel like *Infinite Jest*, Wallace presumed, comprised ambitious and highly educated individuals who had turned previously to advanced art, literature, and social theory for answers to what he once called, in an essay on Dostoyevsky, the "desperate questions" of existence.[10] The novel's challenge may be described as *therapeutic* because it asks those readers to acknowledge the *failure* of these forms of culture to address the sources of their confusion or bewilderment—or, as Wittgenstein would have it, their bewitchment.

This is one way of emphasizing the depth of the affinity between *Infinite Jest* and Wallace's version of Alcoholics Anonymous,[11] which emerges as a *successful* therapeutic model for those within the novel who have been let down, even betrayed, by more fashionable forms of "help." Just as the alcoholic must begin by admitting the failure of her previous attempts to cure herself of her "Dis-ease" (as the veteran AA members like to spell it out for newcomers), so Wallace's novel hopes to compel its reader to recognize that her feeling of "lostness" is connected to her philosophical and rhetorical commitments, as opposed to being addressed by them.

After briefly summarizing the novel's plot, I offer a close reading of the book's famous opening sequence. My hope is that the reading establishes (1) the centrality to the novel's overall ambition of Wallace's engagement with philosophy and (2) the nature of the philosophical problems (or the problems with philosophy) that he wanted his novel chiefly to address. This will set the stage for my discussion of the Alcoholics Anonymous passages, culminating with the novel's final scene, in which Don Gately, our guide to Wallace's AA, lies immobilized on a hospital bed. That we begin the novel in Hal's head and end in Gately's signals where Wallace takes his reader to begin and where he hopes she can conclude.

SUMMARY

The plot of *Infinite Jest* is anchored in the asymptotic narratives of its two main characters, the teenage tennis prodigy Hal Incandenza and the recovering Demerol addict Don Gately. At first, Hal and Gately seem to represent inverse notches on the bell curve of American achievement: Hal is a gifted student-athlete, about to set off a recruiting war between top colleges; Gately is a burned-out former football star, now an orderly at a shabby recovery center down the hill from Hal's school. The setting is a dystopic near-future America where the years are sponsored by multinational corporations—"The Year of the Whopper," "The Year of the Depend Adult Undergarment"—the president is a big-business stooge, and terrorists, bitter at having their land and culture polluted by America, attack with a weapon of potentially mass destruction. Meanwhile, the shell-shocked American public plays sports, watches TV on the fancy new "Interlace" holographic media system, or indulges its addictions in what one of the terrorists refers to as a vast "confusion of permissions" (*IJ* 320).

Preceding the frame of the novel is the suicide via microwave of Hal's father, an avant-garde filmmaker, world-class alcoholic, and the founder of Ennet Tennis Academy, where Hal goes to school and prepares for "the show." As we learn during Hal's farcical sessions with a "grief counselor," Hal had discovered what was left of his dead dad's exploded—Hal's brother Orin calls it "deconstructed" (251)—head in his kitchen, but he had refused except sarcastically to discuss what he'd found with his mother or therapist. As the novel progresses, Hal withdraws from family and friends, taking solace in a secretive daily marijuana-smoking ritual under center court at the tennis academy. He describes himself repeatedly as feeling "empty" or complains that his life seems "theoretical," as in an early dream:

In this dream, which every now and then recurs, I am standing publicly at the baseline of a gargantuan tennis court. I'm in a competitive match, clearly: there are spectators, officials. The court is about the size of a football field, though, maybe, it seems. It's hard to tell. But mainly the court's complex. The lines that bound and define play are on this court as complex and convolved as a sculpture of string. There are lines going every which way, and they run oblique or meet and form relationships and boxes and rivers and tributaries and systems inside systems: lines, corners, alleys, and angles deliquesce into a blur at the horizon of the distant net. I stand there tentatively. The whole thing is almost too involved to try to take it all in at once. It's simply huge. And it's public. . . . High overhead, near what might be a net-post, the umpire, blue-blazered, wired for amplification in his tall high-chair, whispers Play. The crowd is a tableau, motionless and attentive. I twirl my stick in my hand and bounce a fresh yellow ball and try to figure out where in all that mess of lines I'm supposed to direct service. . . .

The umpire whispers Please Play.

We sort of play. But it's all hypothetical, somehow. Even the "we" is theory: I never quite get to see the distant opponent, for all the apparatus of the game. (67–68)

The dream is not just a recapitulation of a certain kind of postmodern metaphor;[12] it is also a critique of it. The problem with the game in the dream, *for Hal*, is not that it is not "real," or interesting, or even that it cannot tell us something about reality. The problem is that it fails to facilitate contact. For "all the apparatus of the game," Hal cannot see his opponent on the other side of the net—and in a sense he does not even believe in him: "even the 'we' is theory." Hal might as well be alone on the court, "twirling his stick." The dream thus emerges as a parable about a game that fails to facilitate communication, one of dozens that are laced throughout *Infinite Jest*, a novel that attempts to communicate with its reader in large part by showing her how far she has been failed by her customary forms of communication, including the brand of literary novel that stops with the description of the contemporary world as "unplayable."

Later on, we learn from Hal's deceased father, who appears as a "wraith" over Don Gately's hospital bed in the novel's closing sequence, that Hal had begun to sink into his anomic malaise even before his father's death, which was why the elder Incandenza had left his son a message in the form of a film. The film had been designed to address the very feeling that Hal describes in the dream. The wraith explains that he had

> spent the whole sober last ninety days of his animate life working tirelessly to contrive a medium via which he and [his] muted son could simply *converse*. To concoct something the gifted boy couldn't simply master and move on from to a new plateau. Something the boy would love enough to induce him to open his mouth and come *out*—even if it was only to ask for more. Games hadn't done it. Professionals hadn't done it. . . . His last resort: entertainment. Make something so bloody compelling it would reverse thrust on a young self's fall into the womb of solipsism, anhedonia, death in life. A magically entertaining toy to dangle at the infant still somewhere alive in the boy, to make his eyes light and toothless mouth open unconsciously, to laugh. To bring him "out of himself" as they say. (838–39)

The father's intent was concomitant with Wallace's own ambition to carry on a therapeutic "conversation" to bring his readers out of *themselves*. But, underscoring the delicacy and risk of such a project, the "entertainment" crafted by Hal's father—called *Infinite Jest*—turns out to be *too* entertaining, immediately paralyzing its viewers with insatiable desire. Literally, they can *only* ask for more. Intercepted by wheelchairbound Quebecois separatists planning to disseminate it en masse to the American public, the film never reaches Hal, who, in the book's opening sequence—chronologically its end—reports that he can no longer make himself understood. What he means is that when he thinks he is talking, his listener registers chaotic animal grunts. It is not immediately clear why this has happened—although two popular explanations are that Hal has somehow seen the film or that his toothbrush had been spiked with an especially lethal hallucinogenic drug. (Much more on this scene below.)

Hal, however, is not the novel's only protagonist, and he fades from the second half of the book in favor of Gately and his grizzled peer group of survivors at Ennet House. Through Gately, the reader is introduced to Boston AA, whose meetings, regulations, and customs Wallace meticulously catalogues. An appropriately skeptical reader is led to wonder when Wallace will puncture the balloon of respect he inflates around "this goofy slapdash anarchic system of low-rent gatherings and corny slogans and saccharin grins and hideous coffee [that] is so lame you just know there is no way it could ever possibly work except for the utterest morons" (350). But, contra much of the criticism of the AA portions of the novel, Wallace finally means to suggest that AA's "corny slogans" are wiser than the condescending witticisms with which we might dismiss them. As a response to despair, the program turns out to be both more serious and more effective than the high-concept entertainment crafted by Hal's father.

The precocious teens at Hal's tennis academy are addicted, too, the novel implies—some to substances and almost all to the individualistic, irony-soaked cultural style that Wallace had described in his earlier fiction and essays[13] and describes again in *Infinite Jest*. This is a world the reader is meant to recognize as her own, only more so. The Recovery Center, an "irony-free zone," represents an "unromantic, unhip" alternative path open to those willing to admit that their "best thinking" has mired them in isolation and pain. It is no surprise that the AA portions of the novel have often been dismissed by critics or interpreted as an index of Wallace's despair with our present condition (Aubry, Konstantinou), since, taken at face value, they seem to challenge directly many of the unspoken pieties of twentieth-century high culture: for instance, its faith in creative self-expression, its contempt for clichés and received wisdom, and its reliance on theory and science-based knowledge as the preeminent forms of understanding.[14] *Infinite Jest*'s "arguments" against these intellectual commitments are not made systematically; they are made through characters like Gately, the novel's supreme embodiment of the AA philosophy. To see Gately as a real hero—and not a parodic or hopelessly compromised one—is to see what is most radical (and also most difficult) about the novel

Wallace has written. And it is the key to understanding in what respect precisely he hoped his novel would be *therapeutic* for his readers.

OPENING WORDS

As a whole, I read *Infinite Jest* as deploying a therapeutic strategy we might call "revaluation." By the end of the novel, readers are prompted to reevaluate their initial assumptions about Hal and Gately—and specifically to arrive at a vantage from which they can see that Gately and his AA brethren have something to teach (although it is not a new *argument*) Hal and his fellow sophisticates at the tennis academy. Taken in isolation, however—as I will take it for the rest of this section—the opening passage of *Infinite Jest* employs a strategy that calls to mind Wittgenstein's notion of philosophical therapy as consisting in a series of illustrations or "examples." Namely, it presents an example, through Hal, of the picture of thinking that is encouraged by what Robert Pippin has called "modern and post-modern self-consciousness."[15]

What are the marks of this sensibility? They are not easily paraphrased (that is part of why we need the example), but, by way of introduction to the scene, it may help to recap some of the sounds of the quarrel between modernism and postmodernism, as artistic movements (in the sense that Burn and Boswell refer to them) but also as philosophies, or what Cavell has called "cultural styles." Very roughly speaking, the hallmark of this quarrel was a debate about the status of the individual and her relation to society, which often shaded into, or depended on, a difference of opinion regarding the possibility of rational agency and the relation between the inner and the outer self. The modern commitment to a pure private space ("I think, therefore I am"; "The point of interest lies very likely in the dark place of psychology"; "All things are inconstant except the faith in the soul")[16] was pitted against the postmodernist diagnosis of—and seeming preference for—total exposure ("We will have to suffer this new state of things, this forced extraversion of all interiority"; "Not only is the bourgeois subject a thing of the past, it is also a myth"; "The soul is the prison of the body").[17]

With this quarrel in mind it might seem perverse to speak of a "modern *and* postmodern" sensibility. If I am right about the opening of Wallace's novel, however, one of its functions is to show how, in the day-to-day trenches of contemporary life, the arguments work to mutually reinforce one another. Indeed, what the combatants have in common—the language and style of the conversation itself—is what is most conspicuous in Hal's opening words. I would like to go through those words carefully, pulling out the sentences I believe to be most indicative of the philosophical "illness" the book as a whole is devoted to treating.

"I am seated in an office, surrounded by heads and bodies."
Infinite Jest opens with Hal, a highly sought-after high-school tennis star, narrating his meeting with admissions officers and deans from the University of Arizona. The meeting has been convened to determine Hal's suitability for an athletic scholarship at the university; its subject is the precipitous falloff in Hal's grades and test scores during his final year at his preparatory high school, Ennet Tennis Academy. It is easy, once one has read the rest of the scene, to retrospectively attribute Hal's choice of opening words to what we are soon to learn about his compromised condition. But this would be to ignore how the words express and invite the reader into that condition. Wittgenstein writes, "The decisive movement in the conjuring trick has been made, and it was the very one that we thought to be quite innocent" (*PI* §308).

Why does Hal not say he is in a room surrounded by other people? Or by administrators from the University of Arizona? Wittgenstein might say that, according to the *picture* that has captivated Hal, there are no people in the room with him, only heads and bodies. ("A *picture* held us captive. And we could not get outside it, for it lay in our language and language seemed to repeat it to us inexorably" [*PI* §116]). In what follows, Wallace will show us how the world comes to look for a person in the habit of describing human beings as "heads and bodies."[18]

"I am in here."
But the opening sentence does not give the full measure of Hal's philosophical picture; for that we are made to wait for the fourth sentence of the novel: Hal's portentous "I am in here." The statement is not in quotations in the text, as if to underscore that we do not know what part of Hal is saying it or who he is talking to. I say it is portentous

because it will be the first statement that strikes us as bizarre. Of course, Hal might simply mean that he is "in the room": the question is why anyone would feel the need to *affirm* such a thing. So we move to a second guess: perhaps Hal means to imply that he is "in" something else—say, his body. The same perplexity then returns at a deeper level, for who would want to insist on *that*? The statement would seem to be redundant, unless it were necessary to insist that we are in ourselves. And where else would we be?

Stephen Burn has argued that *Infinite Jest* "begins and ends with materialism," which he defines as a "monistic thesis that does away with appeals to 'soul' or 'spirit' in its insistence that mind is simply an emergent phenomenon of the biological matter of brain."[19] But Hal's "I am in here" has the opposite sound from this kind of materialism; actually, it would seem to make sense only in a context where materialism presents a threat. Samuel Cohen has accurately described the sense Hal gives in the scene of being "a soul trapped inside a body, literally strapped down, struggling to express himself."[20] "I am in here" is more naturally taken as the opening salvo in Hal's attempt to respond to, or resist, the attempt by gathered administrators to evaluate and define him according to his "record"—that is, his test scores and tennis accomplishments. If Hal can be said in this scene to express a philosophical outlook, it appears to be less reminiscent of materialism than of a Cartesian or dualist response to the *threat* of materialism. The suspicion would seem to be confirmed by the way Hal goes on to talk about his body—as if it were separate from him, distant and alien: "I believe I appear neutral, maybe even pleasant, though I've been coached to err on the side of neutrality and not attempt what would feel to me like a pleasant expression or smile." And then: "The familiar panic at being misperceived is rising, and my chest bumps and thuds. I expend energy on remaining utterly silent in my chair, empty, my eyes two great pale zeros"(8).[21]

Having already registered anxiety regarding the correspondence between inner and outer, Hal now states explicitly that he has been presented with guidelines regarding how he should appear, as if only such guidelines could keep his behavior from descending into obscenity. This coaching, we are led to conclude, was either the result of or has caused Hal's loss of confidence in his ability to communicate his emotions and thoughts. The situation is both exotic and familiar, an extreme rendering of a familiar modern anxiety. The anxiety's philosophical dimension can be stated as follows: how can we ever *know* how we appear or sound to another human being? Hal's "belief" that he appears neutral is stated provisionally, as if waiting for confirmation. But what would be the criteria for confirmation?

> *"You are Harold Incandenza, eighteen, date of secondary-school graduation approximately one month from now, attending the Enfield Tennis Academy."*

As the conversation commences, one of the Arizona deans attempts to summarize Hal's biography. Hal contends that the dean is "a personality-type I've come lately to appreciate, the type who delays need of any response from me by relating my side of the story for me, to me."

Why would Hal appreciate having his "side of the story" related for him, to him? Only, we can assume, because self-expression has become a burden for him. The interview format aggravates the burden at the same time that it raises its stakes: to interview well means to tell one's story successfully, with one's self as the active hero at the center of it. Hal does not want to tell his story. Yet as the meeting continues, Hal grows more and more agitated at the way in which his "story" is being related back to him, including the insinuation that his application has been tampered with or that he is a jock without a brain.

Cohen, in his treatment of this scene, describes Hal as a burgeoning artist with significant affinities to Wallace, whose anxiety can be attributed to the fact that he is undergoing a crisis of expression.[22] But we need not imagine Hal as an artist to express what worries him in this scene. The causes of Hal's anxiety are obvious, and they are described clearly: (1) Hal is unable to "speak up for himself"; (2) the administrators at the college are telling Hal's story for him, to him, but they are doing it clumsily and in a manner he does not wish to affirm. Hal's concern is related to, but bigger than, the local concern that the administrators might "misperceive" what he says; it is, essentially, that they will misperceive who he is.

Such a concern need not have anything to do with Hal's being an artist; although the fact that such linked difficulties—of self-expression and reception—now concern ordinary, educated people, and not just the artist, may suggest a historically specific feature of his problem. The task of self-expression, and of recognition, has been problematic for modern art for some time, but in contemporary society, as Stanley Cavell has noted, it has also become problematic for the "modern man," who feels the burden of finding "something he can be sincere and serious in; something he can mean."[23] How this became a problem for the "modern man" is a long story and not one I can tell here; that it has come to have the *feel* of a deep problem (a deep disquietude, as Wittgenstein would call it) is one of the things Wallace indicates by featuring it so prominently at the beginning of his novel. The stakes of his choosing to do so are high: *Infinite Jest*'s readers' kinship with Hal—and therefore his motivation to delve into this dense one-thousand-page novel—depends largely on their being able to recognize, and be disturbed by, this problem.

Accordingly, Wallace employs various strategies that encourage the reader to identify with—and even admire—Hal, including making him the primary narrator of the scene, thus emphasizing an interiority that would appear to be absent from any other point of view in the room. It even begins to seem a mark of distinction that Hal, in a room full of comparatively corrupt and stupid adults, is so isolated and withdrawn. One of Hal's precursors in *Infinite Jest* is Hamlet, another character who seduces the reader into suspecting that having difficulty communicating one's "inner" self to others is a mark of special intelligence and depth. To be "in here" means in this sense to be protected, special.[24] The reader may suspect that such a man thinks, as Harold Bloom has said of Hamlet, not too much but too well.

Infinite Jest's therapy (like Hamlet's?) will consist in part in the reader's coming to see that what makes its protagonist "special" is also what makes him miserable—and not, or not just, because he sees the world more clearly than his peers.

"Is Hal all right, Chuck? Hal just seemed to . . .
   well, grimace. Is he in pain? Are you in pain, son?"
As questions continue to be raised about Hal's incongruous transcript, Hal's surrogate from the tennis academy—and also his stepfather—C.T. assures everyone that Hal will be a model student and an asset

for the tennis team at Arizona. At that point the dean Hal refers to as "Athletic Affairs" notices that Hal seems to be grimacing in pain. This is the first direct indication that Hal is failing in his coached attempt to "appear neutral." And it is significant that Athletic Affairs reads *pain* into Hal's expression. In *Philosophical Investigations* Wittgenstein uses the phenomenon of pain to illustrate his argument against the coherence of the idea of a private language, inaccessible from the outside. Here the phenomenon is treated from the opposite direction: Hal does not claim to feel pain, yet his outward behavior signals it to those around him. Hal thus seems obscure (say "theoretical") to himself in the way that the one who believes she has a private language imagines herself to be obscure to others. The example, taken flat-footedly, might seem to conflict with Wittgenstein's idea that we can hardly separate our notion of what constitutes pain from the various ways we are used socially to expressing it: here Wallace presents a case, we might say, of "unconscious pain." But, as will become clear, Hal's condition is an abnormal one; and it is precisely the divorce between behavior and intention—the distance between Hal's body and his "I"—that will signal his tenuous position in the human community. (That we would banish—or hospitalize—a person who behaved in such a way is Wittgenstein's point.)

The scene begins to build toward its climax when Hal's surrogates are asked to leave the room so that he will be forced to "speak up for himself." As he prepares to do just that, he reflects on his situation:

> This is not working out. It strikes me that EXIT signs would look to a native speaker of Latin like red-lit signs that say HE LEAVES. I would yield to the urge to bolt for the door ahead of them [DeLint and C.T., who are on their way out] if I could know that bolting for the door is what the men in this room would see. DeLint is murmuring something to the tennis coach. Sounds of keyboards, phone consoles as the door is briefly opened, then firmly shut. I am alone among administrative heads. (8)

The return to "heads" emphasizes the "inexorable" purchase of the novel's opening expression, as well as the fact that Hal's failure of communication with his own body is concomitant with his inability to recognize others as anything other than disembodied or partial. This signals one of the Cavellian and Wittgensteinian themes of the scene and of *Infinite Jest* as a whole. Acknowledgment of the other depends on acknowledgment of the self; if my own head and body appear to me to be disconnected from my "self," then I will likely perceive others also as "heads and bodies," which I cannot penetrate.

Meanwhile, it is symptomatic that Hal's mind deflects into a kind of academic investigation, this time of the word *exit*, before turning to the desire motivating it; *he* wants to leave. Hal does not want to be "in here" anymore.

***"Please just explain to me why we couldn't be
accused of using you, son."***

Although the Arizona administrators worry about various aspects of Hal's high-school record, it is always within the context of one over-arching worry. The overarching worry is that Hal's application is so *obviously fraudulent* that the administrators could be accused of taking advantage of Hal by letting him into the school merely on account of his athletic promise. "Look here," one of them says, "please just explain to me why we couldn't be accused of using you, son. Why nobody could come and say to us, why, look here, a boy so shy and withdrawn he won't speak up for himself, a jock, with doctored marks and a store-bought application" (10).

Importantly, the administrators' concern is not with the possibility that the university might *actually* be using Hal: that they will do so goes without saying. The concern is that the administration might be leaving itself open to being *accused* of doing so. Why share such a concern with Hal? There can only be one reason: the administrators want Hal to help in their (very open) conspiracy to use and exploit him.

This is the context for what we might call Hal's refusal. It is one way of interpreting the scene such that Hal ends up getting exactly what he wants: an EXIT or way out.

"I cannot make myself understood, now."

What Hal says when he is finally compelled to "speak up for himself" expresses his understanding of both the conspiracy and the assumptions that lie behind it: "'I am not just a jock,' I say slowly. Distinctly. 'My transcript for the last year might have been dickied a bit, maybe, but that was to get me over a rough spot. The grades prior to that are *de moi*.' My eyes are closed; the room is silent. 'I cannot make myself understood, now.' I am speaking slowly and distinctly. 'Call it something I ate.'" This last statement, which initially sounds like a non sequitur, calls forth a memory from Hal's childhood. Actually, Hal begins by saying he does not recall what he is about to narrate; his older brother, Orin, has described it to him (10). The memory involves Hal appearing in his front yard as a little boy, having come up from the damp family basement with something "darkly green" on his fingers and saying over and over "I ate this" while holding out "what turned out to have been a large patch of mold." What is truly memorable about the scene, at least for Orin, is the way that Hal's and Orin's mom ("the Moms") reacted to Hal's declaration. "[Orin] remembers her face as past describing," Hal says. "O. says his memory diverges at this point, probably as a result of anxiety. In his first memory, the Moms' path around the yard is a broad circle of hysteria: 'God!' she calls out. 'Help! My son ate this!' she yells in Orin's second and more fleshed-out recollection, yelling it over and over, holding the speckled patch aloft in a pincer of fingers, running around the garden's rectangle while O. gaped at his first real sight of adult hysteria" (11).

A study in hysteria, the memory suggests the first two of what are to be a series of potentially causal explanations for Hal's condition in the college meeting. The condition could be a symptom of physical impairment and thus in some way related to whatever it was that Hal had eaten in the damp basement (later it is suggested that he might have "eaten" something more recently: hallucinogenic drugs). Or its causes could be pop-Freudian—namely, the Moms' hysterical *reaction* to what Hal had eaten, signaling a pattern of trauma and avoidance about to repeat itself in the present. Both of these explanations turn out to be no more than pseudo-explanations, although neither are they chosen at random. Drugs and family trauma are familiar bogeymen for psychological maladies in Hal's cultural milieu.

More proximately, however, the scene foreshadows the response of the adults in the interview room to Hal's personal statement. The

Arizona administrators will respond to what Hal is about to say in roughly the same way as the Moms had responded, according to Orin, to his announcement that he had eaten a piece of mold.

"I am not just a boy who plays tennis. . . . I'm complex." This is Hal's central statement in the scene—we might call it his "statement of philosophy"—and it comes as a direct rebuke to the materialistic accounts of his identity that had been offered by the administrators. It begins with the denial that Hal is just a jock and proceeds into a broader denial of the materialistic or reductionist accounts of his identity that he has been listening to since the beginning of the scene:

> "My application is not bought," I am telling them, calling into the darkness of the red cave that opens out before closed eyes. "I am not just a boy who plays tennis. I have an intricate history. Experiences and feelings. I'm complex.
>
> "I *read*," I say. I study and read. I bet I've read everything you've read. Don't think I haven't. I consume libraries. I wear out spines and ROM drives. I do things like get in a taxi and say, "The library, and step on it." My instincts concerning grammar and syntax are better than your own, I can tell, with due respect.
>
> "But it transcends the mechanics. I'm not a machine. I feel and believe. I have opinions. Some of them are interesting. I could, if you'd let me, talk and talk. Let's talk about anything. I believe the influence of Kierkegaard on Camus is underestimated. . . . I believe Hobbes is just Rousseau in a dark mirror. I believe, with Hegel, that transcendence is absorption. I could interface you guys right under the table. I'm not just a creātus, manufactured, conditioned, bred for a function."
>
> I open my eyes. "Please don't think I don't care." (12)

That Hal delivers such news with his eyes closed offers a hint to how he anticipates it will be received. Apparently in Hal's world such proclamations are thought to be controversial.[25]

But Hal's statement reproduces many aspects of the reductionist account of his identity, even as he attempts explicitly to deny it. After asserting that he has "experiences and feelings," Hal spends the next two paragraphs talking about how many books he has read and his facility with grammar. That is to say: a statement that is supposed to reaffirm his human depth and complexity does not appeal to Hal's being, say, mortal, or loving; it hinges rather on his "interesting" opinions and on his having novel opinions about philosophers. Hal is like the young Hamlet, a student. And what he delivers is, so to speak, a graduate student's defense of his humanity.

But this does not exhaust the things we can say about it, for we can assume that when Wallace inserts philosophers into his novels, he does not do so casually. In his speech Hal names four modern philosophers and a writer of fiction who is often identified with Sartrean existentialism. It could be said that Hal names two dyads of philosophers—Hegel and Kierkegaard on the one hand, Rousseau and Hobbes on the other—often taught as offering opposing notions of the interaction between inner and outer or the individual and society. In ending with Hegel, Hal signals slyly what the novel he is opening will attempt to do—not to settle such long running disputes but to help its reader come to consciousness of and therefore be able to move beyond them. Hal himself, however, has not moved beyond these oppositions; he is rather a product of them. In this scene Hal identifies with his "inside" at the expense of his body ("I am in here," as Kierkegaard might say to Hegel), whereas for much of the book, as a potentially ascendant professional tennis star, he will identify—per the instructions of his tennis instructor Schtitt, a known Hegelian[26]—with his active body over his "empty" inside. The only critic I know of who has noted this "reversal" has accounted for it by asserting that Hal has been the victim of a drug-related prank.[27] This may be the case, although Wallace makes it unconfirmable. Either way, Hal's shift can also be described philosophically, as the consequence of a conversation that has for too long been pulled to extremes, emphasizing either the mind or the body, the inner or the outer. (A variant of this dynamic motivated Cavell to call for philosophy to turn to literature, as if literature had something to teach it about accepting or "acknowledging" the inescapable ambiguity of what he called "the human.")[28]

At the same time that Hal's speech indicates his philosophical intelligence, it suggests the failure of philosophy to help him, *therapeutically* speaking. If it represents a graduate student's defense of his humanity, it also signals the poverty of the version of humanity being defended. If we as readers initially fail to see this poverty, I would propose it is because we share it.

"What in God's name are . . . those sounds?"

The reaction to Hal's speech confirms the completeness of its failure, at least as an act of communication. Having finished speaking, he opens his eyes and looks out. Directed his way is "horror." "Good God," whispers Athletics. Hal hears (it is impossible to know whether anyone actually says it) "*God!*" and "*Help!*" in the room—the same exclamations Orin had told him their mother had made when he had eaten the mold.

"I'm not."

Eventually pinioned by the administrators and dragged out of the room, Hal attempts to reassure himself. " 'There is nothing wrong,' I say slowly to the floor. 'I'm in here.' " Then: "I am not what you see and hear." And finally, "I'm not" (13).

The order of these statements—"I'm in here," "I am not what you see and hear," and "I'm not"—is instructive. The first approaches a classical formulation of Cartesian dualism. It was Descartes who set out to prove, and believed he had proved, "that the mind is distinct from the body," identifying the "self" as the "thing that thinks."[29] The second statement, "I am not what you see and hear," may be taken as an aggravation of the first, denying sharply that what is "in here" can be expressed or properly communicated to others: this is the denial that Hal shares with Hamlet—not only is he "in here," but what is in here seems to him to "surpasseth show." Finally, in the third statement, "I'm not," we have what looks like a negation of rational agency—Hal really has, he realizes now, lost the struggle "to be" in the historically modern sense that Pippin has sketched of "being the subject of one's life"—as well as a kind of surrender to the supposed death of the subject in the age of postmodernism.[30]

Initially, it is hard to see how the three statements could form a continuum: the third seems obviously to contradict the first two. The progression is less surprising if we take the scene to be about the *failure* of dualism as a response to materialism or determinism—or indeed to the skepticism or nihilism that it sees lurking behind those positions. My sense is that the opening scene of *Infinite Jest* dramatizes, philosophically, the inability of the thing that thinks to escape the problems of the body, much less to escape the problem of being perceived as a body—or, say, as "a creātus . . . bred for a function." If Hal's inner "I" is conceived of as a representation of the deep dualist self, then one of the lessons of the scene is that that self cannot survive in total isolation from the world (this is one thing postmodernism is *right* about), just as it cannot bear total exposure to it (what modernism is right about). This is relevant to Wallace's fiction as a whole insofar as he rejected the postmodern taboo against the representation of deep subjectivity, even as he refused to simply return, as many of his contemporaries now have, to the modernist faith in the deep and self-sufficient subject. Hal is not self-sufficient, but the reason we are able to sympathize with him is that he remains, unlike the flat figures that were showing up in the novels of Pynchon, Ellis, or DeLillo, recognizably human—and concerned, as might be expected, by the rumors of his demise.

The fact that such responses failed intellectually to meet the skeptic's challenge, and that they represented failures of humanity, of the human imperative to speak and act without perfect knowledge or certainty, was central to Cavell's attempt to substitute "acknowledgment" for "knowledge" as a criterion for philosophical progress. From this perspective Hal's problem is that, in response to the threat of determinism or, as Burn would have it, materialism, he denies too much. His "I am in here" is not just an announcement of imprisonment; it expresses the picture that imprisons and captivates him. Later in the book Hal will describe one of his great fears as being of "excluded encagement in the self" (694). But the novel as a whole would seem to suggest that the roots of Hal's condition are in his language and therefore in his way of life.

Hal is not *Infinite Jest*'s stand-in for every millennial American, but neither should the trap in which he is stuck appear to be eccentric. His philosophical response to social pressure—the retreat farther and farther into the self—reflects not just an academic but also a popular contemporary notion of subjectivity, perhaps especially prevalent among the demographic most likely to be attracted to novels like *Infinite*

Jest. The opening scene stages the very common modern confrontation between an individual who identifies his most precious self with his inner "feelings and beliefs" and a society that *treats* that human being like an automaton, "bred for a function." The confrontation, Wallace suggests, is mutually reinforcing. The harder the inward-facing individual bumps up against this alienating society (it is symptomatic that as Hal gets more and more uncomfortable, one of the administrators gives the great modern-bureaucratic excuse that they are just "doing our jobs" [9]), the farther he is encouraged to retreat from it, until there can hardly be any communication between what the individual conceives of as his essential self and society at all. This is the sense in which "I am not what you see and hear" is just a stepping stone away from "I'm not." The dynamic is also one way of unpacking the significance of Hal's claim that "Hobbes is just Rousseau in a dark mirror."[31]

What is *scary* about the scene, though, lies not in this theoretical point but in how it depicts human communication—and therefore human community—breaking off and down. We are initiated into its horror if we feel we have some reason to fear such a break—that is, if we fear that we may become, as Hal has become, incapable of describing our "experiences and feelings," much less our pain. That Wallace does not say *how* Hal came to this pass is an aspect of this horror, as if to suggest that to live today is simply to be subject to such breakdowns.[32] Certainly, Hal's intelligence, his vocabulary and grammar, his reading and his interesting opinions have done little to stop it from happening *to him*.

"So yo then man what's your story?"

The opening chapter of *Infinite Jest* ends with Hal being wheeled, or imagining himself being wheeled, down the hallway of a hospital, an orderly "looking down in the middle of some bustled task" and asking, "So yo then man what's *your* story?" (17). Although Hal is in no condition to answer him, it bears emphasizing that the orderly's question is a more inviting, because less hostile, repetition of the earlier line of questioning from the college administrators.

In one sense the rest of the novel will tell Hal's story, affirming his "experiences and feelings" in a way neither he nor the administrators were able to do during the meeting. In another sense critics have agreed that that "story" does not ultimately resolve—as any first-time reader presumes it will—the question of what, in the opening scene, is wrong with Hal. They have tended to see Wallace's refusal to offer such resolution as an invitation to provide their own theory or explanation. So for Hayles the opening scene signifies the puncturing of the illusion of "autonomous selfhood."[33] Frank Cioffi reads it as a part of the book's "disturbing text performance," supposedly aimed at causing readers to virtually experience addiction.[34] And Mary K. Holland interprets Hal's breakdown as signaling the way in which he has been "doomed to the solipsistic death of his pathological society."[35]

Such explanations are not only incomplete or implausible; they do not address what calls most urgently for explanation. First, if Wallace wanted to communicate what Cioffi and especially Hayles and Holland say he wanted to communicate, why would he *begin* the novel with Hal's crisis rather than ending with it? Hayles says that, in such an unorthodox and spiraling narrative, the starting point is largely "arbitrary," but the fact that the meeting in Arizona represents the latest chronological moment in the book surely exacerbates the force of the question of its placement rather than rendering it irrelevant, since it would be customary to put the latest thing last. It is more reasonable to assume that Wallace *opens* his novel with Hal's crisis so it is the first, rather than the last, word on the possibility of "autonomous selfhood" in Hal's "pathological society."

Second, considerations of Wallace's desire for the reader to do a certain amount of "work" notwithstanding, why does Wallace not himself provide a more straightforward explanation for Hal's condition in the course of his novel?

"The clarity that we are aiming at is indeed complete clarity.
But this simply means that the philosophical problems
should completely disappear. . . . When no questions
remain . . . just that is the answer." (Wittgenstein, PI §133)
Glossing this quote from *Philosophical Investigations* in his "Aesthetic Problems of Modern Philosophy," Cavell approaches what he takes to be the "central concept" of Wittgenstein's later work—that is, the notion that "the problems of life and the problems of philosophy have related

grammars, because solutions to them both have the same form: their problems are solved only when they disappear, and answers are arrived at only when there are no longer questions—when, as it were, our accounts have cancelled them."[36] It can be easy to read Wittgenstein's language games as being constructed for other philosophers and even for a certain kind of philosopher: the one who is after an ideal language, for instance. One of the services Cavell does as a Wittgenstein commentator is to bring out an analogy that is sometimes latent in Wittgenstein between, as he says above, the problems of philosophy and the problems of life. This allows a Wittgenstein to emerge who is speaking not only to the philosopher in search of an ideal language but also to the desire within each one of us for certainty and protection, laying bare that desire's personal cost alongside its philosophical one.

Fictional scenes, like language games, can help a reader learn to "account for" the limits of habitual grammar—but fiction is almost unavoidably about life, so the philosophical problem will only come alive if it is simultaneously, even urgently, a practical problem. Hal's predicament in the opening scene of *Infinite Jest* is exemplary in this regard. His practical problem is obvious: communication between himself and his audience has broken down. But the practical problem is, almost as obviously, a symptom of a philosophical problem: Hal's inability to communicate proceeds from his rigidly dualistic picture of his inner/outer self—a picture that reproduces itself in virtually every sentence he (tries to) speak. One of the ambitions of Wittgenstein's later philosophy was to demonstrate the inadequacy, for instance through his private language argument, of the dualistic picture for dealing with the skeptic about other minds. The opening scene of *Infinite Jest* does not reproduce this argument so much as it imagines the consequences for a subject who fails to recognize, or sees no alternative to, that inadequacy.

Consistent with what I take to be Wallace's project as a whole, the scene draws our attention to the power of the threat posed by a society whose assumptions are often materialistic or deterministic, but its aim is to have the reader acknowledge the futility of her most common strategies for responding to that threat. This accounts for the philosophical significance of Wallace's *opening* his novel with Hal's crisis—as if, like one of Wittgenstein's language games, inviting the reader into a grammatical cul de sac—as well as of his leaving it causally unexplained. Although it is irresistibly tempting to look to the rest of the story for clues about what is wrong with Hal, it is also helpful to remember what Wittgenstein meant when he said that a philosophical problem could be solved—that is, that it would "completely disappear." This means not that we would have definitively discovered its answer, or "cause," but rather that, through some change in orientation or perspective, we would have found a way to stop the problem from tormenting us.

I believe that, for the reader who truly understands *Infinite Jest*, the question of how and why Hal arrives at his condition in the opening scene will recede in significance, until it is transcended by a different set of questions and concerns—namely, those raised in the Alcoholics Anonymous portions of the novel and embodied by the novel's other main character, Don Gately.

A CRITIQUE OF THEORETICAL REASON

Although the early part of *Infinite Jest* is taken up mostly with Hal and his fellow adolescents at Enfield Tennis Academy, the book's focus shifts significantly, with much of its final two thirds being set at Ennet House, the halfway house down the street from the school. In those portions Don Gately, who first appears as just one of the many former criminals attempting to recover his sanity at Ennet, emerges as a character who competes for and eventually—if the novel works as I am arguing it does—surpasses the reader's interest in Hal.

Early critical responses to the AA portions of *Infinite Jest* ranged from bafflement to condescension. Some chose not to speak of them at all, as if they represented an embarrassing—and embarrassingly personal, given what is known about Wallace's own addiction issues in his late twenties—foray into a self-help world that can have little relevance for the kind of people that read and analyze novels by David Foster Wallace. Others read the AA portions against what I would argue were Wallace's obvious intentions for them, seeing in AA instructions, for instance, a repetition of the very "recursivity of addiction" (Mary Holland) that the program is supposedly meant to treat.[37]

I will start with two critics—Lee Konstantinou and N. Katharine Hayles—who have taken the AA portions seriously yet, in my view, have mischaracterized the role Wallace's AA plays in the novel as a whole. Although their interpretations are not the same, Konstantinou and Hayles both believe that Wallace's AA is meant in some way to talk readers out of their overdependence on logos or, as Hayles calls it, "ratiocination." For Konstantinou, the AA scenes represent Wallace's attempt to instill the experience of "belief" in his readers, who are portrayed as having become, in the absence of religious faith, variously disillusioned, nihilistic, and skeptical. For Hayles, Wallace's AA is employed as a counterweight to the "power of ratiocination," which has been, in the case of the addict, co-opted by the disease of addiction.

According to my reading, Wallace's AA offers not a way out of or around ratiocination but rather access to a non- or perhaps an antitheoretical *form* of reason. That such a form exists—that is, that there may be rationality and even philosophy that is not theoretical or critical—is one of the hardest lessons of Wallace's AA for some of the characters within the book just as surely as for some of its critics. A way to press this point is to say that if Wallace's AA is antiphilosophical, it is antiphilosophical only insofar as Wittgenstein's *Philosophical Investigations* is antiphilosophical. The profound change it seeks to work in its members could be expressed by the seemingly paradoxical Wittgensteinian claim that "the real discovery is the one that enables me to stop doing philosophy when I want to."[38] (From this perspective Hal's problem in the opening scene is that he is never able to stop doing—a certain kind of—philosophy.)

For Konstantinou, the key to understanding the significance of Wallace's AA is found in Wallace's description of the relationship that AA encourages between its adherents and God—or whatever the individual conceives of as her or his "Higher Power." Konstantinou focuses on the AA directive to Don Gately to go and pray every night, even if he cannot believe in what he prays to—a directive that is consistent with the broader AA instruction: "Fake It Till You Make It" (*IJ* 369). Gately—one of whose virtues as a counselor to new members at Ennet House is said to be his ability to honestly articulate his early difficulty accepting some of the AA directives—confesses that, even after ten months sober, he has trouble with the concept of the Higher Power. Even as he does it, he does not know what exactly he is praying to:

> [Gately's] sole experience so far is that he takes one of AA's very rare explicit suggestions and hits his knees in the A.M. and asks for Help and then hits his knees again at bedtime and says Thank You, whether he believes he's talking to Anything/-body or not, and he somehow gets through that day clean. This, after ten months of ear-smoking concentration and reflection, is still all he feels he "understands" about the "God angle." . . . He feels about the ritualistic daily Please and Thank You prayers rather like a hitter that's on a hitting streak and doesn't change his jock or socks or pre-game routine for as long as he's on the streak. (*IJ* 443)

The ritualistic relationship between the AA adherent and a higher power, Konstantinou says, should be read as a metaphor for the relationship Wallace is trying to build between his reader and the text of *Infinite Jest*. Wallace's goal, according to this interpretation, is to instill a similar kind of contentless "belief" into a readership disillusioned by the deconstructive tactics of metafictionists as much as by such Rortian announcements, popular in Wallace's time if not in ours, that our age is one of banal irony. "Though some critics have interpreted *Infinite Jest* as harshly critical of AA," Konstantinou writes, "we must understand the formal situation of Gately relative to God in terms of the relationship Wallace wants to posit between the reader and belief. That is, belief is not merely a thematic content . . . of the text, but an ethos and an experience it tries to instill in the reader through formal means."[39] Konstantinou takes the appeal to AA to be a sincere failure. The problem, he says, is that Wallace does not consider the social and economic arrangements that have given rise to the ironist, or the nihilist, and thus he offers a merely "symbolic toolkit" against the concrete reality of "bad institutions."

Hayles begins, as does Konstantinou, by chiding critics who do not take the AA portions of *Infinite Jest* seriously, emphasizing that the "immensely hard work of rebuilding subjectivity from the ground up is performed in the story of Don Gately . . . who discovers to his amazement that Alcoholics Anonymous actually works." Next she homes in, also like Konstantinou, on the aspect of AA that she believes forestalls the member's critical faculties:

> Although Gately has no idea why the Twelve Steps have the power to release him from the terrible cage in which he found himself trapped, it gradually dawns on him that he does not have to understand why, only what. Addiction is deadly, he learns, because it infects the will; once reason has been co-opted, it uses the power of ratiocination in the service of the Disease, inventing rationalizations that continue to operate until the Substance kills the Subject. "Analysis-Paralysis," *AA calls this kind of thinking, a state typical of addicts who indulge in making finer and finer distinctions about a situation while failing catastrophically to intervene or act constructively*, a state that Hal often finds himself in after taking marijuana hits."[40]

For Hayles, as for Konstantinou, the goal of AA is to replace "reason" with something else—call it belief or Twelve Steps. That is to say: AA does not represent an alternative form of reason or a critique of a certain form of reason; it represents an end run-around reason, an instruction manual for how to short-circuit it.

A third critic, Timothy Aubry, has offered a modified but still complementary presentation of Wallace's AA, even though Aubry, unlike Konstantinou or Hayles, does interpret Wallace's AA within the horizon of the novel's attempt to offer therapeutic solace to its "self-consciously intellectual readership." Still, Aubry characterizes Wallace's presentation of AA as "ambivalent," approvingly paraphrasing A. O. Scott's pronouncement that "Wallace appears to be no less addicted to the aesthetic habits that he claims to find tiresome than his characters are to various substances." More important, according to Aubry, Wallace signals in passages such as the one Konstantinou quotes above that he is uncomfortable with AA's insistence that its members repeat slogans and clichés to which they may not fully subscribe. "Uttering a slogan whose truth you are not prepared to affirm," writes Aubry, "would seem to be an exemplary instance of irony."[41] And it is this kind of irony of which Wallace himself is guilty, insofar as he laces his novel with platitudes about the wisdom of a program that he himself could not possibly be prepared to endorse the wisdom of.

These three critical responses share certain assumptions, and I take these assumptions to be related precisely to what Wallace found challenging and edifying about the philosophy of AA. Konstantinou and Aubry see that the target of Wallace's critique is not just drug addicts but Wallace's readers, themselves subject to the "extravagant self-conscious, self-doubting, ironic processes undergirding addiction" (Aubry 109). Yet Konstantinou believes that AA can only represent a "symbolic"— and therefore "perverse"—rebuttal to this problem, in the form of an injunction to simply *believe*, while Aubry argues that the goal of Wallace's AA is a nostalgic "recovery of feeling." Hayles sees that AA seeks to address a problem of the will, yet, far from recognizing this as a problem that she, as an academic literary critic, might *share*, she describes it in such a way that its applicability appears limited to the corrupted wills of drug addicts.[42] What binds all three interpretations together is a notion of a single, healthy form of "ratiocination," or reason, which Wallace is presumed to share with said literary critics—and which stands in opposition to AA's pseudo-religious dogmatism. So for Hayles, AA is appropriate for an addict whose reason has been "co-opted" by the disease of addiction, while for Konstantinou and Aubry it offers access to nonrational experiences—of belief or affect—from which Wallace's secular, liberal readers have become estranged.

Wallace does sometimes portray AA as helping its adherents learn how to shut off their critical faculties when necessary. And AA is valued in part for opening its members to certain experiences—empathy, most notably—that are in short supply at, for instance, Hal's tennis academy. If my interpretation of the book is correct, however, the therapy offered by Wallace's AA is aimed at precisely the kind of reader—we might call this reader an *academic* reader, but this does not mean she or he need necessarily *be* an academic—who mistakes a certain picture of critical or analytical thinking for reason *tout court*. Wallace's AA, that is, does not forestall thought or instill belief or sentiment; it offers, rather, an alternative picture of thought, bearing a different kind of respect for the limitations of specifically theoretical reason, including an appreciation of theoretical reason's need for limitation. The reader is invited to see the *similarity* between addicts, who are described at one point as "addicted to thinking, meaning they have a compulsive and unhealthy relationship with their own thought" (*IJ* 203) and the recursive, self-undermining habits of thought of a clever literary sophisticate like Hal. If one way of describing Hal's problem in the opening scene is to return to the dream about the tennis match, where "even the 'we'" has become "theory," then a way of understanding AA's role in the novel is to say that it makes compelling a mode of thought that emphasizes, instead of theoretical sophistication, interpersonal contact, intellectual discipline, and a respect for clear and distinct boundaries, sometimes referred to as conventions. If Hal is an example of "modern and postmodern self-consciousness" taken to a terrifying extreme, the veteran AA members become examples of a sensibility that is not exactly anti-modern, but which recognizes the temptations and potential excesses of modern and postmodern self-consciousness and thus has integrated a set of pragmatic restraints in order to avoid being carried away by those excesses.

In a perceptive article for the *New York Review of Books*, Elaine Blair describes the AA portions of the novel as a "corrective" to the corrosive cynicism about received wisdom practiced by "earlier generations of the American avant-garde."[43] As Blair notes, contra Konstantinou, this corrective is the opposite of symbolic; indeed, the AA scenes allow Wallace to imagine a scenario in which modifying one's habits of thought "might be a pressing matter of survival." Through the often harrowing stories of the addicts at Ennet House, Wallace dramatizes positively precisely what he established negatively through Hal: the potentially life-saving urgency "of simplicity and sincerity, and the potential hazards of overintellectualization and cynicism."[44]

Blair uses something of a shorthand for the way the AA portions of *Infinite Jest* address "overintellectualization and cynicism," which might be misconstrued as according with the view that Wallace's AA is anti-intellectual (although that is not exactly what she says). Yet it is not only by emphasizing simplicity and sincerity that Wallace's AA plays its central role in *Infinite Jest's* philosophical therapy; it is rather by advancing a picture of thought, and of philosophy, that will seem unfamiliar and perhaps initially banal to most of his readers. The idea is not to instill belief in AA, or in anything else, but rather to expose the confusions and limitations of the picture of thinking to which many of Wallace's readers and characters already subscribe. Wallace uses AA not to introduce his readers to a new model of belief but to bring them to consciousness about what they *already* believe.

To make this point more concretely, I will focus briefly on three ways—all laid out from approximately pages 270 to 374 of *Infinite Jest*, when Wallace takes his readers inside Ennet House Drug and Alcohol Recovery House—that Wallace's AA can be said to expose and challenge the sensibility exhibited by Hal in the novel's opening, but with*out* recommending that readers surrender their critical faculties or trade thought for belief or sentiment. Roughly, these will be (1) AA's appreciation for common sense, (2) AA's attitude toward communication, and (3) AA's suspicion of theory.

◆ ◆ ◆

COMMON SENSE. The attitude of Wallace's AA toward common sense can be understood most clearly from the central place it accords to clichés or slogans. It has become a cliché itself for clichés and slogans to be connected culturally with lowest common-denominator consumerism and politically with authoritarianism: the creative writing teacher and the twentieth-century literary critic would seem to agree that the cliché is among the most debased forms of communication. The sophisticated *Infinite Jest* reader's likely hostility toward clichés, already hinted at in Hal's demeaning judgment of the word choice of some of his interlocutors in the opening sequence, is given voice toward the beginning of the section introducing Boston AA by "free lance script writer" Randy Lenz and a professor and the editor of a "Scholarly Quarterly," Geoffrey Day. Lenz and Day are both considered "intellectuals" within the Ennet House community—and it is no accident that Day, during his intake interview, complains that there is "something totalitarian" and even "un-American" about AA's use of clichés (1003n90). Lenz and Day are known for being the most difficult kind of addicts. "It's the newcomers with some education that are the worst," according to one of the intake officers. "They identify their whole selves with their head, and the Disease makes its command headquarters in the head" (272).

Lenz and Day initially express their contempt for AA through their contempt for its reliance on, and lack of suspicion about, clichés. "So then at forty-six years of age I came here to learn to live by clichés," says Day. "One day at a time. Easy does it. First things first. Courage is fear that has said its prayers. Ask for help" (270). To Gately, who listens to Day deliver these sarcastic lectures, "Day is like a wide-open interactive textbook on the disease" (279). "If Day ever gets lucky and breaks down," Gately thinks, "and comes to the front office at night to scream that he can't take it anymore and clutch at Gately's pantcuff and blubber and beg for help at any cost, Gately'll get to tell Day the thing is that the clichéd directives are a lot more deep and hard to actually *do*. To try and live by instead of just say" (273). This is a wisdom that is repeated and reinforced by the novel as a whole, which, despite being often lauded for its verbal originality, is studded with praise for the (sometimes life-saving) consolations of clichés. "Even if they are just clichés," Gately thinks at one point, "clichés are (a) soothing, and (b) remind you of common sense, and (c) license the universal assent that drowns out silence; and (d) silence is deadly, pure Spider-food, if you've got the Disease" (278).

The idea that one might need to be "reminded" of common sense is central to AA, and at first glance it might look antiphilosophical. Isn't philosophy's job to question common sense? According to many analytic philosophers in the Cartesian tradition, yes. But for those familiar with Wittgenstein, the idea cannot but remind them of his conception of the work of the philosopher as "assembling reminders for a particular purpose."[45] This could be a motto for Wallace's AA. AA diagnoses its members as having become estranged or alienated from what we have in common, and pass down to one another, often in the form of clichés. Clichés, that is, become an important vehicle for maintaining and reproducing the form of life encouraged by AA, a form that valorizes what is common and attempts to facilitate it. Lenz and Day, in wanting to tear the clichés out of that form of life and hold them up for ridicule, are analogous to the Wallace critics who have insisted on seeing the clichés within the novel as capable of being held out for analysis—and often for ridicule—without seeing that they are part and parcel of a way of living. This is an eruption of what Wittgenstein would have called bad philosophy, in the midst of AA.[46]

Before moving on, it is worth noting that Gately's defense of clichés is not *merely* pragmatic or functional. Clichés do not just allow the desperate addicts at Ennet House to get through the day; they can also help them to achieve what the book posits as something resembling peace, or grace. "I Didn't Know That I Didn't Know is another of the slogans that looks so shallow for a while and then all of a sudden drops off and deepens like the lobster waters off the North Shore," Gately reflects at one point, adding that such slogans can help "these poor yutzes . . . start to get a whiff of what's true and deep, almost magic, under the shallow surface of what they're trying to do" (271). Wallace does not say much more in *Infinite Jest* about what's under the surface of what the residents at Ennet House are trying to do, though he would pick up on the thread years later in *The Pale King* (see Chapter 4). The point of emphasizing it here is to suggest that Wallace is after more than simply to show his readers how an addict can be taught to hang on. Not just survival, but something that is "true and deep" is held to result from the repeated use of this common or "ordinary" language.

◆ ◆ ◆

COMMUNICATION. As the reliance on clichés goes some way toward demonstrating, the AA community does not always privilege preeminent highbrow values such as originality, creativity, or self-expression. What it does privilege is encapsulated by the name the members give to their nighttime public gatherings: "Commitments." At a Commitment addicts take turns going to a podium and telling their stories— exactly the thing that Hal had found himself incapable of doing at the beginning of the novel. The stories, we are told, share a reliable formula, beginning with the speaker's introduction to his substance of choice, climaxing with his having reached his "bottom," and culminating with his discovery of solace after he "Comes In" to AA. Although some of the AA members initially chafe at the rigid structure, they eventually come to see it as a source of comfort, as they do the rules— some written, some enforced implicitly by the audience—governing language and style. For instance, every speaker begins with the same four words: "I am an alcoholic." After that, they are encouraged to "Keep It Simple." The audience, meanwhile, learns to view jokes, irony, and sarcasm with suspicion—not for aesthetic reasons but rather because they are so well acquainted with their danger:

The thing is that it has to be the truth to really go over, here. It can't be a calculated crowd-pleaser, and it has to be the truth unslanted, un-fortified. And maximally unironic. An ironist in a Boston AA meet-ing is a witch in a church. Irony-free zone. Same with sly disingenu-ous manipulative pseudo-sincerity. Sincerity with an ulterior motive is something these tough ravaged people know and fear, all of them trained to remember the coyly sincere, ironic, self-presenting fortifi-cations they'd had to construct in order to carry on Out There, under the ceaseless neon bottle. (369)

The values around communication at Wallace's AA diverge sharply from those that reign at Hal's tennis academy. The students at the acad-emy are more like Hal's father, the avant-garde filmmaker and head of the academy, who *successfully* passed down to his son an anxiety, and a suspicion, about the possibility of authentic or truthful communication. Wallace himself was critical of writers in the foregoing generation such as John Barth who grew, he believed, more interested in the problem of communication than in actually communicating. For these writers jokes, sarcasm, and self-conscious irony were seen as marks of sophis-tication; in AA the same qualities are known as "self-presenting forti-fications" that allow people to remain isolated from others and indulge in their addictions.[47] But it is worth emphasizing, again, that Wallace's objection to the postmodern focus on communication was not, itself, theoretical. Rather, Wallace attempts to show through the addicts, as Blair suggested, the real-life, concrete consequences of an unchecked propensity toward irony, reflexivity, and double-entendre principles.[48]

If, at the time of *Infinite Jest*'s writing, much of advanced art and criticism had come to seem like the "game" that Hal was unable to play in his dream, Wallace's AA presents a model in which "play" is sharply discouraged. The Commitments, in a Wittgensteinian sense, are also a game, but they are a game in which to play well is precisely to eschew "play." As Gately reflects, this is "harder than it sounds." Sincerity is not a matter *simply* of speaking directly or resisting the temptation to make jokes. As the AA veterans know, any communicative strategy, includ-ing earnestness, can be used with an ulterior motive. There is no way to *theoretically* protect oneself against fraudulence or self-deception.

But this does not mean it is impossible to get better at committing to what one says or that the norm of rhetorical honesty is incoherent or meaningless. "Gately's most marked progress in turning his life around in sobriety, besides the fact that he no longer drives off into the night with other people's merchandise, is that he tries to be just about as verbally honest as possible at almost all times, now, without too much calculation about how the listener's going to feel about what he says" (*IJ* 370). Even here, Wallace's AA expresses realistic expectations—Gately does not pretend he can speak without *any* calculation; he merely acknowledges that there is a point where such calculation becomes "too much."

A second aspect of the AA stance toward communication might be described as its privileging of intention over text. Wallace's preceding generation of postmodern authors were part of a critical and theoretical program that had declared the "Death of the Author"—that is, the death of our interest in the intentions of the author, accompanied by the birth of our exclusive interest in the text. As Day and Lenz demonstrated the prevailing view about clichés, so Wallace imagines a postmodernist critic in the midst of one of the AA meetings, in the form of Joelle van Dyne. Joelle is a late arrival at Ennet, eventually to become a good friend of Gately's but originally connected to the avant-garde art scene through Hal's deceased father (she is said to be the star of the film *Infinite Jest*). Soon after arriving at Ennet, she tells Gately that she finds it "especially hard to take when," at Commitments, "these earnest ravaged folks at the lectern say they're 'Here But For the Grace of God.'" Gately assumes Joelle means she has trouble with the religious aspects of AA and starts to comfort her by confessing his own initial confusion about the Higher Power, but Joelle interrupts him. Her problem is not spiritual, she says, but grammatical:

> "'But For the Grace of God' is a subjunctive, a counterfactual, she says . . . so that an indicative transposition like 'I'm Here But for the Grace of God' is, she says, literally senseless, and regardless of whether she hears it or not it's meaningless, and that the foamy enthusiasm with which these folks can say what in fact means nothing at all makes her want to put her head in a Radarange at the thought that Substances

have brought her to the sort of pass where this is the sort of language
she has to have Blind Faith in." (366)

Gately interprets this speech as involving "Denial-type fortifications
[combined] with some kind of intellectualish showing off." At the same
time, he "doesn't know what to say in reply" and even finds himself
genuinely distressed by Joelle's insight, feeling "a greasy wave of the old
and almost unfamiliar panic" (366). If her goal was disenchantment,
Joelle has been cleverly successful; the speaker's words, here, begin to
seem as if they have been alienated from the people speaking them. And
they threaten to lose their power—even over Gately. By questioning
the text, as opposed to what the text communicates about the speaker's
intention, Joelle has broken a kind of spell—or cast one.

But what does Joelle accomplish with this disenchantment? It might
seem that Joelle here is on the Wittgensteinian side, taking a statement
that sounds deep and cutting it down to size ("literally senseless"). But the
Wittgenstein of the *Philosophical Investigations* could have pointed out
that the sentence's "sense" does not depend on its grammatical or logical
consistency;[49] it depends, rather, on an unspoken agreement between its
speaker and her community of listeners. For the AA adherents at Ennet
House the phrase makes plenty of sense; they no more need "Blind Faith"
than they do analytical tools or grammatical training to grasp what the
speaker means. This is because language is conceived, in Wallace's AA,
as a conduit for intention; if the goal for the speaker at Commitments is
to purify her intentions—to become "verbally honest"—then the audience plays its part by privileging not what was literally said—evaluating
its "logical validity" or judging its originality and cleverness—but what
it thinks the speaker means *by* saying it.

This, as opposed to the relationship between the AA member and
God, is the most revealing analogy between AA and its members and
Wallace and his readers. For that relationship to work, Wallace suggests,
both parties have to value verbal honesty over empty cleverness. To
read the text against its speaker, as Joelle does in the above example, is
not only to miss the point but also to mock and endanger it. It is to be
the witch in the church.

◆   ◆   ◆

THEORY (AND PHILOSOPHY). Konstantinou makes it sound as if Wallace uses AA members to express a theory about the importance of "belief" to everyday functioning, something that is not appreciated by, say, the sophisticates at Hal's tennis academy. But Wallace makes clear that one of the things he admires about AA is that it does not get its authority from its coherence *qua theory*. Indeed, Wallace emphasizes that AA is, on the one hand, analytically mysterious even to those whom it helps ("Nobody's ever been able to figure AA out. . . . It seemed impossible to figure out just *how* AA worked" [349]); on the other hand, it is positively disdainful of attempts to establish chains of causation, since this is perceived as the first move in the theorist's attempt to displace responsibility for her problems onto larger institutional or cultural forces, like family trauma or late capitalism. "So but also know that causal attribution, like irony, is death, speaking-on-Commitments-wise" (370).

It is easy to see how commentators could interpret Wallace as therefore granting, whether approvingly or critically, that AA is hostile toward serious thinking. What I have been arguing is that Wallace's AA advances an alternative picture of serious thinking—in fact, a picture in which much of what passes for serious thought in contemporary philosophy and art is revealed to be little more than (a very dangerous form of) play. I press this point because it has been tempting for Wallace's critics to view his valorization of AA as part of a larger turn in his mature fiction toward mysticism, faith, or "belief." There are moments, indeed, in Wallace's final novel where it would seem he may really begin to creep in this direction. But to take Wallace seriously as a philosophical author involves seeing his endorsement of AA as pointing not away from thinking but toward a picture of it that exposes and challenges our customary one.

As a picture of thinking, Wallace's AA takes its authority from other sources than logical validity or being intellectually provocative—for instance, from the program's practical efficacy and from the community that the shared customs and language engenders. Another criteria is the inner change its adherents report undergoing over time. Gately, we are told, prays to his Higher Power every night not because he wants desperately to believe in something, or because he is convinced by the practice's theoretical soundness, but because the praying does help him to stay sober, day after day, "like a hitter who's on a hitting streak and doesn't change his jock or socks." Why it helps is a question he is not uninterested in but also one he knows may be dangerous to ask too insistently. "The *Why* of the Disease is a labyrinth it is strongly suggested all AAs boycott, inhabited as the maze is by the twin minotaurs of *Why Me?* and *Why Not?*, a.k.a. Self-Pity and Denial, two of the smiley-faced Sergeant at Arms' more fearsome aides de camp" (374). Sometimes the reasonable thing to do is not to ask a question.

At the end of the introductory portion of the novel on AA, Wallace posits AA's "root axiom" as being to "Check Your Head at the Door" (374). Gately knows that this can sound "classically authoritarian, maybe even proto-Fascist," a judgment Hal would probably share with Joelle and the rest. But remember it is only the intellectuals who "identify their whole selves with their heads" (272). That is why it can never occur to them that it might sometimes be rational to "check" one's head—just as it is unlikely to occur to most philosophers how the "real discovery" can be the one that allows them to stop doing philosophy when they want to.

PORTRAIT OF THE ARTIST

Were Wallace ambivalent about what he presents as AA's picture of thinking, a plausible way for him to express that ambivalence would have been to show it failing one of its members at a crucial moment. Instead, he does the opposite, concluding his novel with a portrait of a subject who remains capable of carrying on a "conversation" with his AA community, even under the most dire of external circumstances.

Having been shot in the side while defending some of his charges at Ennet House, Gately finds himself lying heavily and in great pain in St. Elizabeth's Trauma Ward. As at the beginning of the novel, the reader is placed inside the head of a protagonist who cannot speak, but whereas Hal is unable to speak for reasons that are obscure and abstract, there is no mystery about the cause of Gately's silence: Gately has a tube stuck down his trachea. Moreover, Gately, unlike Hal, does not need to be told he is in pain. His pain is not "unconscious." His situation is the more familiar one in which he feels his own pain but does not know how to communicate it:

[Gately] couldn't feel the right side of his upper body. He couldn't move in any real sense of the word. . . . His throat felt somehow raped. (809)

Everything on his right side was on fire. The pain was getting to be emergency-type pain, like scream-and-yank-your-charred-hand-off-the-stove-type pain. Parts of him kept sending up emergency flares to other parts of him, and he could neither move nor call out. (815)

Despite this excruciating pain, what is truly horrible about Gately's situation is similar to what is truly horrible about Hal's: he cannot, at least at first in the hospital room, make himself understood. Like Hal, Gately is moved by his condition to certain philosophical speculations. ("Are they words if they're only in your head, though?" [832]; "What would it be like to try and talk and have the person think it was just their own mind talking?" [833]). Unlike Hal, Gately does not become bogged down in these speculations, and he finds, mostly by reminding himself of AA directives, the resources to check and channel his anxiety. Whereas Hal's speculations led him down a rabbit hole that had exacerbated his personal crisis, Gately has developed a method of thinking that helps, rather than hinders, his adjustment to his predicament. Gately, too, is in danger of being thought of in the hospital as "just a body"—not least by the doctors who want to prescribe him painkillers despite his personal history. Philosophically speaking, the difference between his and Hal's responses to their situation may be described as that between a dualist response to a materialist threat and a Wittgensteinian or a Cavellian one.

The proof of AA's effectiveness as a picture of thinking is finally shown, appropriately, not through any explication of its theoretical foundations but in its practical efficacy for Gately. The climax of the novel's final scene consists in Gately's epiphany that the key to enduring his pain lies in his ability to *resist* the temptation to theorize about it:

No one single instant of it was unendurable. Here was a second right here: he endured it. What was undealable-with was the thought of all the instants all lined up and stretching ahead, glittering. . . . It's too much to think about. To Abide there. But none of it's as of now real. What's real is the tube and Noxzema and pain. . . . He could just hunker down in the space between each heartbeat and make each heartbeat a wall and live in there. Not let his head look over. What's unendurable is what his own head could make of it all. What his head could report to him, looking over and ahead and reporting. But he could choose not to listen; he could treat his head like G. Day or R. Lenz: clueless noise. He hadn't quite gotten this before now, how it wasn't just a matter of riding out the cravings for a Substance: everything unendurable was in the head, was the head not Abiding in the Present but hopping the wall and doing a recon and then returning with unendurable news you then somehow believed. (860–61)

Whereas for both Hal and the formerly drug-addicted Gately, pain was rendered somehow unreal or theoretical—one of the advantages of drugs, Gately remembers, is that "pain of all sorts becomes a theory, a news-item in the distant colder climes way below the warm air you hum on" (891)—here Gately acknowledges that "what's real is . . . pain." What is "unreal" is what Gately knows his head is capable of doing with the pain—that is, of "looking over and ahead and reporting." But Gately recognizes, per AA, that he "could choose not to listen" to his head. We might say that this is precisely the choice that never occurs to Hal.

Whereas Hal, with all faculties intact, is unable to communicate with the Arizona administrators, Gately gradually finds ways to communicate with those who come to visit him in the hospital, even without words. Of course, Gately is confronted with a more sympathetic audience—the kind of audience whose expectations have been educated by the AA "Commitments." One after another, Gately's friends from Ennet come to share their stories and offer him words of encouragement. His first desire to speak out loud is sparked when he wants to tell his friend Tiny Ewell that he can "totally fucking I.D." (815) with a story Tiny shares from his childhood. When his AA sponsor, Ferocious Francis, drops by, Gately wants to explain to him "how he's discovered how no one second of even unnarcotized post-trauma-infection-pain is unendurable. That he can Abide if he must" (885). At one point he scribbles signs into a notebook to make sure the doctor doesn't put painkillers in his I.V. (888); at another he gestures to show Joelle that he sympathizes with something she says to him, reflecting that "it makes him feel good all over again that Joelle had understood what he'd meant. She hadn't just come to tell her troubles to somebody that couldn't make human judgment-noises" (884).

The point is not just that Gately conquers his anxiety about communication, whereas Hal succumbs to it, but that Gately and Hal want different things. This is because, perceptually speaking, they inhabit different worlds. Hal's world is impersonal, judgmental, suspicious. The Arizona administrators are there to evaluate him, a process with which he is more than familiar from his time at an elite prep school. That he describes himself repeatedly as being "alone" in the room underscores the extent to which he has been coached to stay within himself ("in here") even when around other people. Hal finds his "exit" from the situation, but it is an exit into a privacy that is inseparable from madness. For Hal, the only way out is to retreat further in.

In the world of Gately's hospital room, by contrast, the prevailing expectations are for empathy, identification, and endurance. Far from feeling judged by those who come to visit, Gately worries that they will mistake his inability to speak for an incapacity to sympathize. Far from feeling himself to be alone, he worries that his conversational partners will feel that *they* are alone. The problems of intention and reception that seem so intractable to Hal are here conceived of as practical rather than theoretical or metaphysical. This is what allows Gately to succeed where Hal and his father—Wallace's stand-ins for a line of experimental artists who could never, so to speak, *get over* such problems—both fail. For Gately, too, communication has become difficult, but he does not inflate that difficulty into something more mysterious or interesting than it is. Wallace follows his lead insofar as his own experiments within *Infinite Jest* can be viewed as aiming not at alienating or mystifying his audience but simply at getting through to it.

KINDS OF THERAPY

In his book *Reading as Therapy* Timothy Aubry describes *Infinite Jest* as having a therapeutic intent, by which he means that the novel represents an endorsement of conventional therapeutic culture, adapted to the needs of Wallace's "self-consciously intellectual readership."[50]

Although I agree that the book is therapeutic, I see Wallace's therapy as being more than merely a more intellectual version of conventional "talk therapy." To maintain this distinction, it is helpful to refer to *Infinite Jest*'s own representative of conventional therapy, the "grief counselor" hired by Hal's mother to help him deal with his father's death. Characteristically, Hal views his time with the counselor as an obligatory contest of wits, and he earns his freedom from the relationship once he figures out what the therapist wants to hear.

The literary-philosophical therapy that Wallace enacts in his novel is not wholly unrelated to the procedures of psychoanalysis, but it is not concerned with answers; rather, it is aimed at helping us see the senselessness of our questions. As Cavell summarizes it:

> It is my impression that many philosophers do not like Wittgenstein's comparing what he calls his "methods" to "therapies" (§133); but for me part of what he means by this comparison is brought out in thinking of the progress of psychoanalytic therapy. The more one learns, so to speak, the hang of oneself, and mounts one's problems, the less one is able to *say* what one has learned; not because you have *forgotten* what it was but because nothing you said would seem like an answer or a solution: there is no longer any question or problem which your words would match. You have reached conviction, but not about a proposition; and consistency, but not in a theory. You are different, what you recognize as problems are different, your world is different. ("The world of the happy man is a different one from that of the unhappy man" [*Tractatus*; 6.43].)[51]

A novel that subscribed to a conventional, pop-Freudian variety of therapy (I call it "pop" to distinguish it from the more complicated matter of what Freud actually believed) would have culminated with a discovery of what had caused Hal's crisis in the interview room: perhaps it was his relationship with his father or the episode his brother remembers involving the mold and Hal's mother. *Infinite Jest* does not follow this model; in fact, it includes disquisitions on the grave dangers of "causal attribution." Instead, it begins by introducing its reader to one world—the world of Hal's tennis academy—and it ends with the reader having been introduced to a different world, with different problems. The book does, as Kakutani complained, leave its reader "suspended in midair." But the point of its open-ended structure is not to provoke critical detective work; it is rather a matter of, or a model for, a certain kind of philosophical procedure. The reader of *Infinite Jest* is left with the sense that one set of problems—say the problems of adolescence or of postmodernism—has, without ever being solved, been superseded by another—say the problems of maturity or of life. As always, from the vantage point of the second set of problems, the first will have come to look imaginary or fantastical.

That *Infinite Jest* is a work of *philosophical* therapy is evident precisely in the fact that it does not compel its readers, as Aubry suggests, to "connect" with their feelings but rather to come to terms with the philosophical presuppositions and habits that could have ever led them to feel that they were "disconnected" from them in the first place. I have argued for the various ways in which Wallace's AA is *methodologically* philosophical, but Ennet House is also philosophical in its *aim* insofar as its guidelines are engineered to get its members to distinguish real from false desires, concrete from imaginary needs. This is a classical task of philosophy, although one from which it is easily distracted. It is also one of the main tasks of *Infinite Jest*. If the novel's therapy has been successful, the reader does not emerge with (for instance) a new and improved theory of communication but rather a sense of conviction about a world where communication is an everyday human problem, capable of being addressed with the right blend of creativity and common sense, rather than an abstract or a theoretical one that leads into anxiety and darkness. We might say that *Infinite Jest* seeks to bring communication "back from [its] metaphysical to [its] everyday use."[52]

Such an interpretation can be accused, as Wittgenstein imagines someone saying of his *Philosophical Investigations*, of "destroy[ing] everything interesting, that is, all that is grand and important" about *Infinite Jest*. Yet, as Wittgenstein responds there, "What we are destroying is nothing but houses of cards"—that is, phantoms that we had invested with a fantastical importance.[53] To be disabused of such fantasies is not to be clear of suffering, as the troubled souls of Ennet House are no doubt meant to testify. Still, to repeat Freud's wisdom as a paraphrase of the journey that *Infinite Jest*'s reader takes from Hal's consciousness to Gately's: "much has been gained if we succeed in turning your hysterical misery into ordinary unhappiness."[54]

So Decide

Brief Interviews with Hideous Men as Philosophical Criticism

You don't have to think very hard to realize that our dread about both relationships and loneliness . . . has to do with angst about death, the recognition that I'm going to die, and die very much alone, and the rest of the world is going to go merrily on without me. I'm not sure I could give you a steeple-fingered theoretical justification, but I strongly suspect a big part of real art fiction's job is to aggravate this sense of entrapment and loneliness and death in people, to move people to countenance it, since any possible human redemption requires us first to face what's dreadful, what we want to deny.

—David Foster Wallace, "An Expanded Interview"

We have got on to slippery ice where there is not friction and so in a certain sense the conditions are ideal, but also, just because of that, we are unable to walk.

—Ludwig Wittgenstein, *Philosophical Investigations*

IN A WIDELY CIRCULATED April 2017 post for the website *Electric Literature*, entitled "Men Recommend David Foster Wallace to Me," Deirdre Coyle describes her resistance to reading Wallace's fiction, based mainly on the insistence with which her male colleagues and boyfriends have recommended it to her. For the sake of the article she finally agrees to read Wallace's collection of stories, *Brief Interviews with Hideous Men*. Instead of writing directly about any of the stories, however—"it's been written about enough," she says—Coyle reflects on what it feels like to have a book by a "straight cis man about misogyny" recommended to her over and over by straight cis men. Do these men not realize that she already knows about misogyny? "I understand that maybe other men wouldn't absorb the message unless it was being told to them by another, probably smarter and better educated man," Coyle concludes, "but then why do men keep recommending his work to me?"[1]

Coyle's article makes explicit several questions about subject matter and audience that have been central to the reception of Wallace's collection of short stories since its publication in 1999. One of the book's first reviewers, Michiko Kakutani of the *New York Times*, mused that although the collection was presented as a "sardonic commentary on our narcissistic, therapeutic age," the stories were as "tiresome and irritating" as their target.[2] Likewise, in the *New York Review of Books*, A. O. Scott wondered whether, in view of the collection, Wallace's fiction could be said to represent "an unusually trenchant critique of [the] culture [of narcissism] or one of its most florid and exotic symptoms."[3] (His answer: both). In 2016 the literary critic Amy Hungerford objected, like Coyle, to the implication that she should read the book at all. Recounting an interaction with an editor at the *Los Angeles Review of Books*, who recommended that, if she wanted to publish an article accusing Wallace of misogyny, she should "engage a bit with the 'Brief Interviews with Hideous Men,'" Hungerford comments that "this editor assumes that Wallace's work 'about' misogyny must somehow be revealing or smart about that topic."[4]

Such judgments are not difficult to account for given the book's subject matter and style. The stories in *Brief Interviews* are convoluted, repetitive, and often grotesque. Some, like the metafictional sendup "Octet," are dense with footnotes and a cold, academic vocabulary; others—especially the eponymous "Brief Interviews"—can seem merely mean-spirited or engineered to shock the reader with the ugliness of the behavior they depict. It can easily appear that Wallace is offering little more than a tour into the theme park of the educated male psyche, a location already duly ransacked by the past century or so of white male writers. Revelations about Wallace's own misogynistic and even abusive treatment of women constitute yet another challenge to any critical recommendation of *Brief Interviews*. As Hungerford implies, there is reason to doubt that someone who has been guilty of misogynistic behavior will be able to offer meaningful wisdom about misogyny.

I propose that a different evaluation of the stories is possible, if one takes seriously the idea that one of art's jobs, therapeutically speaking, can be to "aggravate" our sense of entrapment (or "encagement," as it's called in *Infinite Jest*), to encourage us to "face what's dreadful" about life in general or our lives in particular. The stories in *Brief Interviews* can indeed be "tiresome and irritating"—and for those who do not believe themselves to be touched by the problems it addresses, they may also appear indulgent or redundant. Nor do I think we should assume that they have any wisdom to offer about misogyny; in fact, it would be prudent to enter into the stories with some foreboding on this score. Contra Coyle's claim that *Brief Interviews* has been endlessly analyzed, however, there have actually been few attempts to describe how the collection's various parts fit together or how the book interacts with the rest of Wallace's oeuvre. My goal in this chapter will be to return the discussion to the book itself, which is the only place where the question of how Wallace's personal misogyny may have affected his writing about misogyny can be adjudicated.

To be sure, *Brief Interviews* appears at first to be darker and less redemptive than *Infinite Jest*; there are few "ethical countertypes" to be found in it, and its subject matter is, as I have mentioned, almost relentlessly repulsive. It is no accident that some critics, even long before the public accusations about Wallace's treatment of women, have been eager to distance themselves from the book's "florid and exotic" subject matter (as Scott called it). But this critical tendency toward distancing may itself be revealing. After all, it is far easier than countenancing the possibility that the hideous men are the endpoint of "our" way of speaking, thinking, and writing—that is, are products of a pervasive historical and intellectual environment, or of the response to that environment, that is often treated as the most sophisticated and serious. Indeed, Coyle's and Hungerford's implication that the book's treatment of intellectualized misogyny is tiresome in view of their own life experiences supports the idea that there is nothing particularly "exotic" about the type of character with which the book is concerned. I hope to show that it is so common that, to see the book rightly is to see that, while not all of us are hideous men, almost none of us are untouched by the cultural, social, and philosophical dynamics the hideous men both expose and embody.

ONE NEVER KNEW

Brief Interviews combines semiconventional short stories with vignettes, epiphanic think pieces, a couple of long monologues, and an ongoing series of fictional interviews, arranged like selections from a broken-off field study and appearing as answers to questions signaled by a "Q," followed by a blank line. On its face it makes no claim to being any more unified than any other collection of stories that may simply have been written within a certain period or published in similar kinds of magazines. As with Wittgenstein's *Philosophical Investigations*, there is no third-person narration or commentary to tie its various vignettes and free-floating "interviews" together. Similar also to the *Philosophical Investigations*, however, the several elements of *Brief Interviews* appear to be addressed to a recurring set of problems, or "temptations," that occur in a specifically demarcated historical and social milieu. Marked as occurring on page 0, the short vignette that begins the collection establishes some of the pressing features of that milieu:

> *A RADICALLY CONDENSED HISTORY OF POSTINDUSTRIAL LIFE*
> "When they were introduced, he made a witticism, hoping to be liked. She laughed extremely hard, hoping to be liked. Then each drove home alone, staring straight ahead, with the very same twist to their faces.
>
> The man who'd introduced them didn't much like either of them, though he acted as if he did, anxious as he was to preserve good relations at all times. One never knew, after all, now did one now did one now did one." (0)

The vignette appears to be set at a dinner party or small social gathering, where people come to make "connections." It is the kind of event at which one might be consumed by the self-conscious query that frames the interaction between the man and the woman: will I be liked? When Hegel said that art, after the end of Art, would be concerned with the contingent trivialities of modern bourgeois individuals, he may have had in mind scenes like this. But it is to misread Wallace to see him as calling nostalgically for a return to a time—call it preindustrial or premodern—where the questions of mundane social life might have seemed less urgent. For the most part Wallace joins the Western modernists, and some of the postmodernists, in situating his fiction in a thoroughly disenchanted social world. As in the novels of Virginia Woolf or Henry James, what motivates the characters in *Brief Interviews* is not some transcendental or political project but rather the "basic human need [for] some sort of connection" with other people (*BI* 258). If such a need has become particularly urgent in postindustrial modernity, not to mention unprecedentedly complicated to satisfy, this is all the more reason for a writer like Wallace to take it seriously.

Yet there *is* something under attack in *Brief Interviews*. Chief among the differences between Wallace and some of his modernist and postmodernist forebears is that Wallace is not content to *reflect* contemporary alienation in his fiction; he wants therapeutically to "treat" it. The result is that whereas in much of twentieth-century literature loneliness or isolation are presented as signs of special sensitivity to the problems of modernity, or society, or existence—we might think, respectively, of Musil's Ulrich, Pynchon's Slothrop and Camus's Meursault—here they appear as both deriving from and contributing to a pervasive confusion. What is under attack in *Brief Interviews* as a whole will be a certain way of talking and therefore of living, which seems to exacerbate the problems of postindustrial life—social atomism, the fear of fraudulence and inauthenticity—under the pretense of addressing them. This is why it is significant how the vignette ends up, with both of the introductees, having attempted to act in such a way that they would be liked, driving home alone, that peculiar "twist" on their faces. Meanwhile the host, "anxious … to preserve good relations at all times" (0), reveals that he dislikes both of the people he has just introduced.

This all risks seeming trivial or being simply derivative of the brand of sharp and cynical social observation that we find in John Updike, John Cheever, and Richard Yates. And it is not immediately clear that it has anything to do with history or philosophy: that concluding "One never knew . . . " could refer merely to the host's uncertainty about the course of social life, in which you may, after all, come to depend on someone tomorrow whom you can do without today. As the coda to an opening vignette that claims to be a history of postindustrial life, though, the concluding statement would seem able to bear further analysis. Wallace would hardly be the first to consider it a genuine insight of, as well as a genuine problem for, postindustrial life that *one never knows*. That is one of the consequences of the various intellectual revolutions, having brought with them the destabilization of traditional knowledge and normative authority: we do not know who we are, why we are here, what our purpose is, even (as Descartes said) whether we are here, awake, sitting by the fire, and so forth. Centrally for the book we are about to read, this epistemological uncertainty has often become linked to, or developed into, a social uncertainty that presents itself to us as the puzzle of whether we can really *know* another person. In academic philosophy this is named the "problem of other minds"; for Wallace's characters it manifests itself in a question they feel with a special urgency: do "other people deep inside experience things in anything like the same way you do" (*BI* 136)?

In his book on Henry James, Robert Pippin situates James's achievement as related to the refusal, in the face of the uncertainty of modernity, to become simply a moral skeptic. James's novels, Pippin says, reflect and investigate the myriad ways in which free, modern subjects, in the shadow of the breakdown of normative authority, continue to create and feel compelled by a newly emerging set of socially negotiated norms and values. The difference in the world the reader is plunged into in *Brief Interviews* is not so much with the historical or metaphysical situation—that uncertainty, and whatever forces of secularization, industrialization, and so forth seem to have caused it, is still pervasively there—but with the set of responses that seem available and tempting to the author's characters. Wallace is separated from James by a century of artists and academics (indeed, by the rise of whole academic departments that are devoted to) exploring and addressing, with more and more confidence and insistence, the contours of the new social world that was beginning to emerge in James's fiction. The result is that Wallace's hideous men do not share the innocence or the hesitancy of James's or Woolf's characters in the face of an encroaching modernity; rather, they give the impression of being "well-versed," not only in the nuanced cultural conventions that have come to stand in for the old authorities but also in the semiotic codes that govern how they are expected to talk about those conventions.

I raise this issue here because it might seem, in what follows, that I'm treating two very different kinds of problems—one set of which is applicable primarily for artists and intellectuals, the other for ordinary citizens of modernity. My claim is that Wallace's collection is valuable in part for emphasizing the connection between what might seem to be artistic or philosophical problems with uncertainty—both social and epistemological—and much more practical or everyday modern difficulties. This connection is sometimes brought out via analogy; more often, though, Wallace shows through the juxtaposition of characters and situations the manner in which the ordinary modern person has become enmeshed in difficulties surrounding self-knowledge and communication that may at one time have been thought to affect only artists and philosophers. This is why it is significant that, besides offering a succinct statement of the bourgeois, capitalistic, historical situation, the opening vignette also contains a dramatic critique (a critique *through* dramatization) of the way two ordinary modern people respond to that situation and that their responses can be so easily mapped onto strategies familiar from twentieth-century art. One can romanticize uncertainty, as some modernists did (hence the slightly enervated poetry of that final line—"one never knew . . . "); one can attempt conservatively to mitigate its worst consequences, say, shoring fragments against our ruin, as the host attempts to do with his talk of "preserving good relations," and one can make "witticisms," as the man does at the beginning, coolly ironizing that uncertainty—that is, the postmodern response.

All three kinds of responses to the modern fact of uncertainty are addressed in the collection, but Wallace does the most to develop and "aggravate" the response of the guests who drive home alone, which he considered most characteristic of the advanced art and academic thinking of his time. Many of the "hideous men" who appear in the stories to follow resemble sophisticated postmodern rhetoricians, psychoanalysts, and literary theorists, skilled in the art of "unmasking" the root causes of antisocial behavior, both others' and their own. "Much of the annoying, pedantic jargon I use to describe the rituals also derives from my mother," says interviewee #48, having earlier ascribed his habit of tying women to his bed to a "desire symbolically to work out certain internal complexes consequent to my rather irregular childhood relations with my mother and twin sister" (*BI* 94, 88). In interview #2 a man attempting to rationalize leaving his girlfriend admits that, given his pattern of prior abandonments, he "might be a psychopath" (*BI* 84). In interview #28 two men debate the question of what contemporary women "want," acknowledging that this is a complicated matter in part because

> today's postfeminist era is also today's postmodern era, in which supposedly everybody now knows everything about what's really going on underneath all the semiotic codes and cultural conventions, and everybody supposedly knows what paradigms everybody is operating out of, and so we're all as individuals held to be far more responsible for our sexuality, since everything we do now is unprecedentedly conscious and informed. (*BI* 195)

In many regards the two men name acutely the historical situation of the audience Wallace was addressing—and they do so in the casually academic language that audience may be presumed to associate with sophistication and forward thinking. Yet the passage indicates something paradoxical: learning how to talk knowingly about the unmasking of cultural conventions is not the same thing as knowing how to go on in their absence. Diagnosis is not the same as cure, and in some cases—for instance, when the diagnosis is fetishized or comes to seem like an end in itself—it can impede it. Read back against the opening vignette, the passage suggests the primary criticism Wallace's collection will make of what its characters consider the most sophisticated approach to social life. Postmodernism, the men theorize, is the time when "supposedly everybody . . . knows everything" about cultural conventions and paradigms. That "supposedly" indicates the skepticism with which these men regard this postmodern "truth"; yet their own way of talking would seem to enmesh them in it. They can admit, rhetorically, that we only "supposedly" know everything, but even this is presented as a bit of analytical knowledge, which the men cannot allow to lay the groundwork for a form of life where the fact that "one never knows" would be actually lived with, as opposed to being ironized, romanticized, or denied. The men grant the insufficiency of theory—-but only theoretically.

This is a familiar predicament throughout the collection, where men frequently express cynicism about, or ironically distance themselves from, a form of speaking they cannot seem to abandon. One senses that in this case, as in many others, the men's explanation of their predicament has been inefficacious even if accurate; it is not necessarily mistaken so much as their reliance on it reveals their entrapment within a certain way of talking and therefore of thinking.

This can lead us to address, at least provisionally, what Wallace considers really hideous about his hideous men. The adjective has many meanings, and there are superficial ways in which some of the hideous men will register to the reader as simply physically ugly or cruel. But what strikes us as hideous in every sense of the word (i.e., monstrous, repulsively unnatural, morally ugly, etc.) about the man who constantly leaves his girlfriends is not that he finds it hard to commit—a common human difficulty—but rather his attempt to justify this difficulty in a language that grows progressively more abstract and generalized. Similarly, the "pedantic jargon" of the man who ties up his dates, his articulate but ultimately self-serving self-awareness about the sources of his proclivity, only exacerbates the contempt we feel for him.

Likewise the two men discussing what women "want" make several insightful—in the purely academic sense—observations about the situation of contemporary women, yet there is something ugly, I think we are meant to infer, about two men discussing this topic in the manner that they do *at all*. The truncated interview #36 helps us fill in what that something is:

"So I decided to get help. I got in touch with the fact that the real problem had nothing to do with her. I saw that she would forever go on playing the victim to my villain. I was powerless to change her. She was not the part of the problem I could, you know, address. So I made a decision. To get help for *me*. I now know it was the best thing I've ever done, and the hardest. It hasn't been easy, but my self-esteem is much higher now. I've halted the shame spiral. I've learned forgiveness. I *like* myself."

Q.

"Who?" (*BI* 28)

The exchange is designed to show how, even if the man's description of his self-growth is in some sense accurate, it condemns him to a kind of moral error, insofar as it transforms a woman who was once close to him into a stepping-stone for a self-justificatory personal narrative.[5]

Moving to the literary level—which the collection continuously encourages us to do—this is an intellectual habit Wallace sees the metafictionists and the postwar realists (or "great male narcissists," as he once called them)[6] to share. In the case of the realists it is a well-worn complaint that the women in the novels of Bellow, Roth, Updike, and Mailer are often simply pawns and punching bags for the men.[7] Meanwhile Patricia Waugh defined the metafictionists as a group of writers who endeavored to "explore a *theory* of fiction through the *practice* of writing fiction."[8] Politically, of course, the metafictionists were opposed to what was seen as the retrograde misogyny and solipsism of the realists, yet—as Wallace's collection implies—many of their own methods, as well as their prevailing focus *on* method, risked impressing readers with a complementary form of self-regard. From the point of view of philosophy, fiction or narrative had traditionally been the art form that honored particularity, but in the hands of the metafictionists it became complicit in philosophy's habitual disregard for the particular. The hideous men are often storytellers. But they are united by an inability to tell a particular story without theorizing about or abstracting from the story they are telling.

Wallace can be accused of doing the same thing; indeed, he self-consciously hales from this tradition, and this is part of what Scott and Kakutani accuse him of when they point out that his collection represents both a diagnosis and a symptom of a certain contemporary sickness. One might think, after all, that the reasonable response to the observation that literature had grown too reliant on an abstract and theoretical vocabulary would have been to produce a work of emotionally earnest or "sincere" fiction similar to what Wallace is often thought to have called for in his early essay on television.[9] This is not the route Wallace took, for reasons that, I have been arguing here, have to do with his commitment to fiction as a form of philosophical therapy. The point was not to inspire his readers with a vision of a completely different form of life, which may in fact remain inaccessible or alien to them, even if they admire it. Rather it was to get them to consider, via a series of aggravating examples, the confusions intrinsic to their own. This was one way of acknowledging that such confusions were not the result simply of obtuseness, or of individual psychology, but of something that lies at least as deep as the language we seem compelled to use to describe them. Part of the project of bringing *Brief Interviews* "to consciousness of itself" is, I take it, to bring forward the background against which the hideous men speak. Accordingly, I turn next to two stories that begin to articulate the philosophical causes, and consequences, of the social uncertainty that is the subject of the Radically Condensed History.

FOREVER BELOW

Following the condensed history of postindustrial life, there are two short pieces depicting male characters at the sides of pools. The first, entitled "Death Is Not the End," observes a highly decorated "fifty-six-year-old American poet"; the second, entitled "Forever Overhead," concerns a boy celebrating his thirteenth birthday.[10] If the condensed history describes the historical predicament of Wallace's characters, and some artistic responses to it, these two stories outline what might be called their philosophical predicament, alongside two kinds of philosophical response to it.

The poet's story, often taken to be a satire of Updike, Philip Roth, or John Ashbery, is told in one three-page paragraph in the third person. The poet sits "reading his magazine in his chair on his deck by his pool behind his home" (3). Thinking back on his myriad awards and fellowships, as well as the one fellowship of which he was unjustly deprived (the Guggenheim), the poet is conspicuously, even extravagantly, alone. He does not make any movement to get into the pool; the "whole enclosed tableau of pool and deck and poet and chair and table and trees and home's rear façade is very still and composed and very nearly wholly silent" (3). The stillness and enclosedness of the poet's environment reflects an inner condition of decadent self-satisfaction, which Wallace depicts as stagnant or lifeless. Iannis Goerlandt says that "one of the points the story makes is that the end lies in this stasis, not in death itself."[11] The story's title, "Death Is Not the End," is most naturally taken as referring to the artist's desire for immortality through art. But it is precisely this desire, Wallace implies, that causes death to come *before* the end. Paradoxically, the artist's desire to stand apart and transcend finitude or death will lead him to create dead or lifeless art; after all, there is only one way—as Cavell would say—to escape the human.

This story represents, then, a solipsistic and therefore doomed response to the problem of uncertainty—one presuming that art—that is, language—is capable of rescuing us from it. Rhetorically, the story discourages identification or empathy such as to reproduce the feeling of distance and alienation that the poet both invites and relishes.

The next story, in contrast, immediately invites the reader to put herself in the protagonist's place, even to consider herself *as* the protagonist. "Happy Birthday," the story begins. "Your thirteenth is important. Maybe your first really public day. Your thirteenth is the chance for people to recognize that important things are happening to you" (4).

The thirteenth birthday, of course, reflects a turning point or an initiation; here it is marked also for its proximity to puberty and adolescence and thus to the emergence of the kinds of desires and fears that can lead to the passion for isolation expressed by the acclaimed poet. Already, the boy is reckoning with the costs and complications of his newfound desires: "This afternoon, on your birthday, you have asked to come to the pool. You wanted to come alone, but a birthday is a family day, your family wants to be with you. This is nice, and you can't talk about why you wanted to come alone, and really truly maybe you didn't want to come alone, so they are here" (5). The boy had wanted to come alone; the boy can't talk about why he had wanted to come alone; the boy is not sure he actually wanted to come alone. But although he has ultimately accepted the company of his family, there is still something the boy has determined to do alone—"You have thought it over. There is the high board" (6).

The thing the boy has to do alone is dive into the public pool, which prompts us to consider what the public pool represents for him. First, the boy thinks, the public pool "is a system of movement. Here now there are: laps, splash fights, dives, corner tags, cannonballs, Sharks and Minnows, high fallings, Marco Polo" (7).[12] But the boy does not want to think about this *too* much. "Get out now and go past your parents, who are sunning and reading, not looking up," the narrator advises him: "Forget your towel. Stopping for the towel means talking and talking means thinking. You have decided that being scared is caused mostly by thinking. Go right by, toward the tank at the deep end. . . . A board protrudes from the top of the tower like a tongue. Each of your footprints is thinner and fainter. Each shrinks behind you on the hot stone and disappears" (7). The metaphors begin to pile up. If the diving board is like a tongue, then what does that make the public pool? One of the cultural developments that Zadie Smith reads *Brief Interviews* as responding to is "philosophy's demotion into a branch of linguistics."[13] Is the boy's dive meant to dramatize a leap into language? Or is to jump off a tongue meant to mark one's escape from (private) language? Or does the dive, at the precipice of manhood, represent a decision about what the boy will have to say for himself? And why, again, should he do it alone?

This question becomes tied up with the question of how the boy will confront his newfound appreciation for the consolations of solipsism or solitude. If the poet by his pool has settled in, comfortably, to his isolation, the boy sees solitude all around him, as a temptation and a trap. Getting in line for the diving board, he notes that "few talk in the line. Everyone seems by himself" (8). But when he gets to the top of the board, he spends a moment reflecting on the attractions of being by oneself: "The late ballet below is slow motion, the overbroad movements of mimes in blue jelly. If you wanted you could really stay here forever, vibrating inside so fast you float motionless in time, like a bee over something sweet" (12).

Smith has interpreted "Forever Overhead" as marking Wallace as a "moralist," someone for whom what mattered was "not the end but the quality of our communal human experience before the end . . . what passes between us in that queue *before* we dive."[14] I agree that this story, as with most of Wallace's fiction, has a moral aim. But

I suspect Smith has drawn the wrong moral from "Forever Overhead." Her formulation suggests that the dive off the board represents a dive into death, whereas the thrust of the story implies that the dive is into life—that is, into finitude, society, and history. To stay up on the board, "forever overhead," is the desire of the poet by his pool or the philosopher by his fire. The boy is marking his first taste of the temptation to remain outside of time, as if poised theoretically above it "like a bee over something sweet." Being alone up on the board has its pleasures, chief among them the pleasure of a great "view" (12); to remain forever overhead is to remain—alone—in a place where death is not the end. The pool, however, represents what he calls the "forever below." But never does he imagine this as a lifeless or dead location. Rather, he thinks, "forever below is rough deck, snacks, thin metal music, down where you once used to be; the line is solid and has no reverse gear" (13).

Such a description of "forever below" might seem to only reinforce one's desire to stay forever overhead. And, in a sense, it does. But the boy, although he is by himself up on the board, has not come to the pool alone. Standing on the board, he realizes that "forever below" is not only bad music and existential finitude but also his family ("a birthday is a family day"). Below lies the whole social world of attachments and mortality and love. "So which is the lie? Hard or soft? Silence or time? The lie is that it's one or the other. A still, floating bee is moving faster than it can think. From overhead the sweetness drives it crazy" (13). The sweetness is the sweetness of the external world, and that sweetness will, eventually, draw the boy into it. But the affirmative jump into the public pool—"The board will nod and you will go, and . . . that is forever" (13)—requires the boy to let go of something. It requires he let go of a conception of the self that can remain impassive and private, forever overhead, watching.

In the rest of *Brief Interviews*, what it means to be hideous, or morally ugly, will correlate closely with the inability to let go of this overhead, self-conscious self—a self that is "scared" by thinking, but even more scared by admitting the limits of certain kinds of thinking. The point is not simply how the boy conducts himself in line before he dives but *that* he dives, something the poet in his yard had never even considered doing. Put another way, the boy's achievement is to refuse to be immobilized by his realization that thinking cannot *solve* the problem of whether he should dive or not.

This does not mean that the boy *simply* acts or *simply* takes a leap of faith, for the story also warns against the opposite extreme: "It may, after all, be all right to do something without thinking, but not when the scariness is the not thinking itself" (10). As with the AA sections in *Infinite Jest*, the stories of the poet and the adolescent and pools in *Brief Interviews* dramatize a choice not between thought and action, faith or belief, but between different forms or habits of thought, including habits that allow one to keep from being overwhelmed or paralyzed by one's thoughts. Such a recognition is necessary to resist the suspicion, voiced most prominently by Smith in regard to *Brief Interviews*, that Wallace advances faith as an alternative to intellectual analysis or that he considers all forms of self-consciousness equally deleterious. Wallace is a self-conscious writer, hardly hostile to the modern project of self-knowledge. But the stories in *Brief Interviews* remind us that "explanations"—the form of thinking that Wittgenstein and Cavell associated with modern philosophy after Descartes—come to an end somewhere: in this case, at the end of a tonguelike board. And after an explanation comes to an end, what we are left with will be a decision—though not necessarily a blind one. ("Did you think it over? Yes and no" [13].) "Forever Overhead" concludes with this final instruction and salutation:

> . . . Step into the skin and disappear.
> Hello. (13)

To step into the skin of the pool is to step into a new skin, to be reborn, as in a baptism, except the baptism requires acceptance not of God but of one's dependency and mutual entanglement with the world. The "hello" welcomes the boy, as it welcomes the reader, to a home—call it modernity—where uncertainty, dependency, not to mention finitude ("there's been time this whole time" [12]), will have to be acknowledged, just as a condition of really living there. The pool is also the stories. What Wallace is asking of his readers is that they submerge themselves in the stories, which means that they be willing to risk stepping out of their own skin ("Happy Birthday"). To meet the stories on their own terms is not merely to mark Wallace's procedures but to allow oneself to be marked by them.

GOOD WILL

For Wallace, any investigation of the form of life of his "hideous men" had also to be an investigation of the literary and theoretical arts that both shaped and reflected that form of life. This is why, at the very center of his collection,[15] he places an experimental exercise that emphasizes the similarity between the communicative uncertainties facing the fiction writer or artist and those confronting the ordinary modern individual—the kind of self-conscious individual who worries at parties not only about whether he will be liked but also about whether others can tell he's worried about whether he'll be liked, and so on.

Formally, "Octet" is one of Wallace's most complicated experiments. It begins as a series of "pop quizzes," echoing John Updike's "Problems" but with some relevant differences.[16] Each quiz depicts discrete interpersonal situations calling for a moral "decision" on the part of one or more of the protagonists. The decisions look disparate but are unified in the sense that we have difficulty figuring out how to judge them: none can be evaluated according only to their practical outcomes or by any strict theoretical criteria. Nor can the right decision be reached by referring to prevailing rules or conventions, for such norms are either absent or they clash with one another such as to render them practically useless. Indeed, each scene can appear designed to reveal the decision to be not, as Wittgenstein would say, a problem of the intellect but one of the will. This means making the "right" choice hinges not on the application of principle but on the exercise of a moral virtue, such as courage, trust, or compassion.

The first quiz is in one sense the simplest and in another the most enigmatic. Entitled "Pop Quiz 4," it tells the story of two "late-stage terminal drug addicts [who] sit against a wall in the cold on January 12, 1993" (*BI* 111). Only one of the drug addicts has a coat; the other appears "gravely ill." The one with the coat stretches it as far as it can go over both of them. At the end is the question: "Which one lived?" (111). The question is bizarre and obviously unanswerable, and the quiz itself might seem an outlier given that the ones that follow it all trace complex moral conflicts, whereas this concerns a simple act of compassion. I think it is meant to introduce in the simplest form possible what Wallace takes to be involved in making a moral sacrifice for another person. As in every other case in "Octet," the question is not intended to prompt an answer but rather to remind the reader of something. In this case it reminds us that, in sharing his coat with the gravely ill terminal drug addict, the other terminal drug addict has exposed himself; that is, he has literally risked his life.[17] The use of the word *terminal* underscores how late in the day it is for both men and that they are both going to die soon—a fact that itself makes the question somewhat ironic. Yet the irony of the question does not mitigate its ability to evoke the outlines of a sensibly Kantian moral universe: it is possible even in the darkest of circumstances, the story suggests, to act with either a selfish or a generous will.

What follows PQ4 are a series of more subtle moral conundrums (a woman who has to choose between raising her baby in poverty and abandoning it to her ex-husband's repugnant but incredibly wealthy family; a man attempting to hide from his wife how much he loathes her dying father) in which, nevertheless, the moral question seems to hinge on a capacity for the kind of sacrifice that, while explicitly a sacrifice for someone else, also requires the sacrifice of a treasured self-conception. But one of these conundrums is abandoned in midstream—"the whole *mise en scene* here seems too shot through with ambiguity to make a very good Pop Quiz, it turns out" (113)—and in a footnote the narrator describes several other protoquizzes that never made it into the published story. The question of what exactly constitutes a good pop quiz has therefore been raised even before the announcement of PQ9, which begins with an abrupt shift of perspective—or, say, of responsibility:

> You are, unfortunately, a fiction writer. You are attempting a cycle of belletristic pieces, pieces which as it happens are not *contes philosophiques* and not vignettes or scenarios or fables, exactly, though neither are they really quantifiable as "short stories." . . . Maybe say they're supposed to compose a certain sort of "interrogation" of the person reading them, somehow—i.e. palpations, feelers into the in-

terstices of her sense of something, etc. . . . . though what that "some-thing" is remains maddeningly hard to pin down, even just for your-self as you're working on the pieces . . . (123)

The immediate effect of this second-person address, echoing the second-person opening of "Forever Overhead," is to shift the reader's burden from attempting to answer or "figure out" the riddles posed by the previous "interrogations" to imagining herself *as* a fiction writer—one who is attempting to produce such a cycle. As this writer, "you" are told that you had set out to write an octet, composed of eight situations that would together convey some "ambient sameness" in human rela-tions. You had immediately realized that five of the eight pieces didn't work at all, "meaning they don't interrogate or palpate what you want them to, plus are too contrived or too cartoonish or too annoying or all three" (124). You were left with the previous PQs. At this point you tried to read the octet "objectively" and figure out if, in its fragmented form, it was meaningful. Yet this turns out to be an extremely difficult question to answer; after all, the pieces are obviously meaningful to *you*, the one who wrote them. How can you be sure they will be meaningful to your reader?

The problem of other minds is thus raised here in the form it would most likely take for a literary artist. But even *thinking* about this ques-tion puts you, as a fiction writer, perilously close to trying to figure out if the reader will "like the octet," and "both you and the very few other fiction writers you're friends with know that there is no quicker way to tie yourself in knots and kill any human urgency in the thing you're working on than to try to calculate ahead of time whether that thing will be '*liked*.' It's just lethal":

> An analogy might be: Imagine you've gone to a party where you know very few of the people there, and then on your way home afterwards you suddenly realize that you just spent the whole party so concerned about whether the people there seemed to like you or not that you now have absolutely no idea whether you liked any of them or not. Anybody who's had that sort of experience knows what a totally lethal kind of attitude that is to bring to a party. (Plus of course it almost always turns out that the people at the party *didn't* actually like you,

for the simple reason that you seemed so inbent and self-conscious
the whole time . . .) (130)

In the "radically condensed history of postindustrial life," a set of aesthetic and philosophical problems could be inferred from the depiction
of an everyday social situation; here the analogy works the other way
around, locating what may seem like an "artistic" problem in a mundane
social interaction. The party brings again to mind a contemporary setting where people are attempting to be liked, then traces two ways in
which this endeavor can fail. First, the person consumed with whether
she will be liked will fail to actually get to know any of the other people
at the party, presumably "driving home alone" like the man and the
woman in the opening vignette. Second, this person will not, even on
the most superficial level, succeed in coming across as likable.

A solution to this problem might seem to be to deny that the judgment of others has anything to do with who we are or what we mean—
that is, to decisively privilege our "inner" selves over the self that we
expose to the public. But this option, sometimes associated with romanticism or modernism in the arts, is connected in *Brief Interviews* to the
temptation to remain "forever overhead," like the decadently isolated
writer in "Death Is Not the End" or the boy poised on the edge of the
diving board. Insofar as it tends to reinforce the very isolation we turn
to other people to escape, it is neither possible nor advisable, Wallace's
story suggests, to dispense entirely with the question of what others will
think. Solitude amounts to an attractive way of denying the problem of
other minds—we might say, of other people—as opposed to a durable
way of addressing it. The writer, like any other citizen of modernity,
must find some way of taking into account whether what she does will
be meaningful to a world of people that do not live inside her head. This
is why the challenge at the center of the collection is simultaneously
philosophical, literary, and social: how, as contemporary individuals,
to acknowledge our need for the approval of others without becoming
that need's victim.

But the problem of other minds might be approached in another
way: perhaps, instead of worrying silently about whether everyone at
the party likes you, you could acknowledge your insecurity, and the
artificiality of the party setting, by going up and *asking* other people at

the party what they think of you! This, Wallace indicates, is the so-cial/aesthetic wager of the literary-philosophical movement that was popular among advanced artists during his education as a writer in the 1980s: the movement known as metafiction. Metafiction, that is, presents itself as one way of "puncturing the fourth wall" and allowing an artist to "be with" his audience without becoming its prey. "Because now it occurs to you that you could simply ask her. The reader . . . whether she's feeling anything like what you feel" (130–31). It is this thought that prompts you to create an appendage to the octet, PQ9, which would be "a kind of metaQuiz." The metaQuiz would, you hope, find a way to address the problem of interpersonal uncertainty. Yet the author of "Octet" points out that such a strategy is far from foolproof. In a footnote he relates that the strategy of stepping back from some-thing and commenting self-reflexively—sometimes taken to have been invented by sophisticated postmodern novelists—had filtered into pop culture decades ago to such an extent that it is sometimes referred to as "The Carson Maneuver," based on how Johnny Carson used to "sal-vage a lame joke by assuming a self-consciously mortified expression that sort of metacommented on the joke's lameness and showed the audience he knew it was lame" (135n17). Anyone who undertakes the strategy of metacommentary these days has therefore to reckon with the possibility that it "may well be that all it'll do is make you look like a self-consciously inbent schmuck, or like just another manipulative pseudopomo Bullshit Artist" (135).

The key to avoiding this fate, says the narrator of the story, is that "you're going to have to eat the big rat and go ahead and actually use terms like *be with* and *relationship* and use them sincerely—i.e. without tone-quotes or ironic undercutting or any kind of winking or nudging" (132n9). In other words, you're going to have to be really sincere, or "naked," in your employment of metacommentary. Yet this opens you to the opposite danger: not of being seen as a manipulative "Bullshit Artist" but of coming across as overly credulous and sentimental. At *best*, the quiz (and the story) concludes:

> It's going to make you look fundamentally lost and confused and
> frightened and unsure about whether to trust even your most fun-
> damental intuitions about urgency and sameness and whether other

people deep inside experience things in anything like the same way you do . . . more like a reader, in other words, down here quivering in the mud of the trench with the rest of us, instead of a *Writer*, whom we imagine to be clean and dry and radiant of command presence and unwavering conviction as he coordinates the whole campaign from back at some gleaming abstract Olympian HQ.

    So decide. (136)

Before evaluating what Wallace is saying here, at the end of PQ9, it is worth pausing over the question of what he is *doing* by including such a quiz in the octet in the first place. PQ9, remember, is both part of the octet and stands outside of it as a kind of commentary. As commentary it describes some of what the previous pop quizzes have in common; but by presenting PQ9 as part of the quiz, Wallace suggests that, whatever the previous quizzes share with one another, they must *also* share with PQ9. The "ambient sameness in different kinds of human relationships" (124), that is, extends to the relationship between the fiction writer and the reader that is described in PQ9. This means that, if they are going to have a successful relationship, both the writer and the reader will have to make sacrifices—similar in kind if not in degree to the sacrifice that the terminal drug addict makes to the other terminal drug addict in PQ4.

Here at the end we finally get a sense of what Wallace thinks this sacrifice consists of. As the philosopher Stephen Mulhall puts it in his essay "Quartet: Wallace's Wittgenstein, Moran's Amis," Wallace

aspires to write in such a way as to "be with" his readers, to meet them as equals on the common ground of their lostness and confusion and self-doubt; and the idea of the Authoritative author makes this impossible. Hence he aspires to write in such a way as to do without—to disavow or sacrifice—this immensely comforting self-image, and thereby to encourage his readers to do without its foundational role in their self-image as well; for both parties, this will amount to a radical kind of dying to the self (as that self is presently constituted).[18]

Whether the sacrifice that is being called for—of authority on the writer's side, idolatry on the reader's—really amounts to a "kind of death," as Mulhall and also Wallace imply, is debatable; the broader point of marking what is required of both is to suggest that writing is (no more or less than) a form of communication like many others, fraught with many of the same risks (pretension, sentimentality, misunderstanding) and promising some of the same potential benefits (connection, inspiration, acknowledgment). The author is not some separable entity, of the kind that could "die"—as in the Barthian, postmodernist conception—or be transformed into a faultless authority—as in the Joycean, modernist one—but a human being attempting to communicate something she considers to be of importance.

Yet this only begins to address the question of what the reader is ultimately being asked to decide. As Mulhall reads it, "So decide" is "something between an order and a reminder."[19] I take it that Mulhall means to evoke Wittgenstein's conception of a "reminder," in the sense that "the work of the philosopher consists in marshaling reminders for a particular purpose."[20] That would lead us to consider what the "purpose" is of this reminder. Yet at just this point Mulhall breaks off his interpretation of the story to note that the reader is less likely to seriously consider how to deal with these authorial problems (she is not, after all, an author) than to "decide" whether what Wallace is doing constitutes "one more shallow, dissembling and hypocritical metatextual exercise— . . . or . . . an unprecedentedly explicit, pervasive and sophisticated way of acknowledging the primacy of the reader's imagination."[21] By posing this question at the end, Mulhall joins his reading with that of the critic Adam Kelly, who, in an essay on Wallace and sincerity, interprets that "So decide" as indicating that "in an era where advertising, self-promotion and irony are endemic, the endpoint to the infinite jest of consciousness can only be the reader's choice whether or not to place trust and Blind Faith."[22]

For both Mulhall and Kelly, then, the decision at the end of "Octet" amounts to a power transfer from Wallace to his readers, with the readers being asked to "decide" whether Wallace is being sincere in turning over this power to them. Both observations connect back to Zadie Smith's suspicion that "how you feel about 'Octet' will make or break you as a reader of Wallace, because what he's asking is for you to have faith in something he cannot ever finally determine in language: 'the agenda of the consciousness behind the text.'"[23] What Smith means is that "Octet" is so dense, enigmatic, and potentially obnoxious that, unless readers have faith in the agenda behind it, they will give up on it—that is, refuse to work out whatever its appeal is to them, assuming instead that Wallace has simply invented yet another literary mechanism for talking to himself. And it is true that "Octet" has often been treated in Wallace criticism as a limit case, exemplifying for the critic either the richness and moral urgency of Wallace's project or that project's hopelessly pretentious and convoluted moralism. The recent revelations about Wallace's personal conduct toward women will only raise the bar for those disinclined to trust the "agenda of the consciousness" behind this text.

But to the extent that Mulhall, Kelly, and Smith all consider the "decision" at the end of the story as a referendum on *Wallace*, they reinforce the very framing of the author-reader relationship that the story is designed to therapeutically undermine. The reader has been asked, at the very beginning of PQ9, to imagine that he or she is a fiction writer. In arguing that the reader, not actually being a fiction writer, is unlikely at the end of the story to maintain this perspective, Mulhall betrays his own lack of confidence in Wallace's procedure, his own refusal to step into its skin. For when Wallace begins PQ9 by saying that "you are, *unfortunately*, a fiction writer" (emphasis added), this need not strike us as merely a speculative pronouncement. Indeed, if we can resist the academic urge to read the sentence metaphorically, we might linger over what it would mean to actually imagine the extent to which it is true. After all, the modern person really *is* confronted by many of the same kinds of problems, and the same kinds of opportunities, that are confronted by the modern fiction writer. And this condition—as readers, as writers, as human beings—*is* unfortunate, at least from the perspective assumed by most of the characters in Wallace's collection, who picture it as a deficiency of their form of communication that it cannot be made immune to misunderstanding.

Metacommentary is thus revealed as a tool of communication—nothing more and nothing less—that the modern individual can use to "puncture the fourth wall" (*BI* 134) if she so chooses. Yet the phrase "fourth wall" itself represents an example of the kind of language we habitually use to insinuate that the challenges facing the artist are matters primarily of technical expertise—with Brecht, for instance, as a professional scaler of such walls. Wallace does not deny that art poses technical or theoretical challenges, but these are not, the author of "Octet" seeks to impress on his reader, its chief challenges. "So decide" is a reminder in the form of a command. The command is for the reader, as the writer, to decide on a strategy of communication, but the reminder behind the command is that decisions about communication, artistic or otherwise, cannot be divorced or isolated from decisions about human relationships. Metafiction, just like any other literary strategy, might make the author look "100% honest," or it could make him look like "just another pseudopomo Bullshit Artist." Nothing about the metafictionist's method necessarily challenges our picture of the author as an authority, yet this does not mean metafictional strategies might not be useful for a writer who truly does want to emphasize the commonalities between author and reader. Meanwhile from the point of view of the reader, whether to trust the agenda of the consciousness behind a text is here revealed as a decision just like the decision to trust, as far as we dare, another person. The therapeutic recommendation on both sides is to confront our doubt and skepticism without denying or trying to "solve" them—not to stop thinking but to stop denying the limitations of what a certain form of thinking can decide for us.[24] This means recognizing the role that decision and mutual dependency inevitably play in modern human relationships, whether between two terminal drug addicts sitting against a wall or between a writer and a reader of an experimental collection of stories.

"Octet" thus resolves into a therapy, not a theory. Having brought its readers, in part by asking them to think of themselves as writers, to the rhetorical impasse that makes metafiction seem attractive, the story shows self-reference to be as haunted by the threats of inauthenticity, and fraudulence, as the conventionally realistic "illusions" it had promised to supplant. This does not mean every artist that undertakes such a strategy is a fraud, only that we deceive ourselves insofar as we think our method of communication can ever protect us from the *possibility* of fraudulence. Wallace himself, as will be seen in the next story, does not carry on by calling for a prereflective form of writing or even by joining what was sometimes trumpeted in his name as the fiction of the "new sincerity." In fact, the darkest story in *Brief Interviews* is precisely about both the attractions and the inaccessibility of simple sincerity—the polar opposite of self-conscious metafiction.

LET ME EXPLAIN

If "Octet" is an exploration of metafictional strategies of self-reference as a potential solution to modern, social uncertainty, the collection's final interview, "B.I. #20," stages a confrontation between that way of communication and another form of rhetorical "openness." The interview is with a man who claims to have been transformed by precisely the kind of "earnest" or "sincere" story that one might have thought Wallace would have tried to write, given his objections to theory's influence on fiction. The story itself, however, is related to the reader secondhand, by a "hideous man" who believes it holds the key to his own moral redemption. This should make us immediately suspicious of his claims that he was "moved, changed" by the story he retells— and this suspicion will, ultimately, prove to be justified. At the same time, it is important not to underestimate, simply based on his ugliness, the extent to which the man's problems represent a therapeutic aggravation of our own.

The story begins with a declaration of love, delivered as if *in medias res* and related to another story—ostensibly about rape:

B.I. #20 12-96

New Haven CT
And yet I did not fall in love with her until she had related the story of the unbelievably horrifying incident in which she was brutally accosted and held captive and very nearly killed.

Q.
Let me explain. I'm aware of how it might sound, believe me. I can explain. In bed together, in response to some sort of prompt or association, she related an anecdote about hitchhiking and once being picked up by what turned out to be a psychotic serial sex offender who then drove her to a secluded area and raped her and would almost surely have murdered her had she not been able to think effectively on her

feet under enormous fear and stress. Irregardless of whatever I might have thought about the quality and substance of the thinking that enabled her to induce him to let her live.

"Everything seems to be played out," says Christoforos Diakoulakis,[25] in this story's opening lines, which announce both the end result of the interviewee's encounter with a woman—he fell in love with her—and also the precipitating cause of this end result: she told a story of having been raped and almost killed. In the ensuing paragraphs the interviewee fills in the blanks. The interviewee—possibly a Yale graduate student: hence New Haven, and his frequent recourse to academic jargon—met and "picked up" a woman at an outside concert ("the pickup itself [was] ... almost criminally easy"); the woman came home with him and they had sex; the interviewee had been planning to leave the woman with a fake number in the morning (she was a "strictly one-night objective") until she told him "the story of the unbelievably horrifying incident" in which she had convinced a dark-skinned rapist in a pickup truck not to kill her (246).

It is noteworthy that the interview begins, as it will end, with the interviewee attempting to explain how the woman's harrowing story affected *him*. The beginning also prepares us, subtly, for the role of "the story" (the story-within-the-story) in "B.I. #20." The interviewee says he is going to "explain" how he fell in love with the woman, but his explanation consists primarily of the story that the woman told him.[26] The cause of his love is not only the content of the story but also, even predominantly, the form or manner in which she tells it, which caused him to fall in love with her. Repeatedly, the interviewee interrupts his recounting of the woman's story to deliver details about her style of presentation. "She was not melodramatic about it . . . nor affecting an unnatural calm the way some people affect a natural nonchalance about narrating an incident that is meant to heighten their story's drama and/or make them appear nonchalant and sophisticated"; "she was, or seemed, oddly unposed for someone this attractive and with this dramatic of a story to tell"; "She seemed . . . open to attention but not solicitous—nor contemptuous of the attention, or affecting disdain or contempt, which I hate"; "she seemed, quote, sincere in a way that may in fact have been smug naiveté but was nevertheless attractive and very powerful in the context of listening to her encounter with the psychopath" (*BI* 253).

It is as if the woman has found the way out of the maze of "Octet," able to offer her story nakedly—she is literally naked, on the man's bed, as she tells it—and yet avoiding the potential pitfalls of melodrama, condescension, manipulative self-consciousness, and posing that had been said to haunt metafiction. Her sincere delivery, the interviewee reports, helped him

> focus almost entirely on the anecdote itself and thus helped me imagine in an almost terrifyingly vividly realistic way just what it must have *felt* like for her, for anyone, finding yourself through nothing but coincidence heading into a secluded woody area in the company of a dark man. . . . It was tribute to the—her odd affectless sincerity that I found myself hearing expressions like *fear gripping her soul,* unquote, as less as televisual clichés or melodrama but as sincere if not particularly artful attempts simply to describe what it must have felt like, the feelings of shock and unreality alternating with waves of pure terror. (254)

As with the AA members in *Infinite Jest*, the interviewee here gestures toward a renewed appreciation for clichés and for our everyday ways of describing things—as if to emphasize that we have forgotten, or lost touch with, the effectiveness of our common, everyday language. Yet as throughout the interview—and unlike in the AA portions of *Infinite Jest*, which are mostly told through the eyes of a nonintellectual—the interviewee also communicates a coldness and skepticism toward the woman. Even when attempting to praise her, he registers his hesitation: "[it] may in fact have been smug naiveté"; her expressions were "not particularly artful"; "Irregardless of what I might have thought about the quality and substance of the thinking." It is symptomatic that nearly every observation is modified by the suspicious—but ubiquitous, in academic locution—verb *seemed*.

This paradox runs throughout the interview. Explicitly, the interviewee claims to have been "moved, changed" by the woman's story and particularly by his realization toward its end. The woman ultimately forms a "soul-connection" with her rapist, thereby short-circuiting the method by which he typically dehumanizes and then destroys his victims. The rapist still rapes her, but he leaves her alone in the woods and does not kill her. The interviewee is brought by this story to what he presents as a devastating piece of self-knowledge: his approach to women was hardly any better, or less empty, than the rapist's. Yet his self-consciousness, his use of the word *quote* before words like *sincerity*, and his skepticism about the interviewer's ability to understand *him*— "I can't make you feel what I felt"; "I will not even try to explain it to you"; "I was moved, changed—believe what you will" (269–70)—tell an altogether different story.

At the end of the woman's narrative, the interviewee recounts, she "indulged in" a moment of commentary, mentioning "that her whole life had indeed led inexorably to that moment when the car stopped and she got in, that it was indeed a kind of death, but not at all in the way she had feared as they had entered the secluded area" (270). We are not told enough about the woman's life either before or after the incident—itself a telling omission—to do anything more than speculate about how the experience with the rapist could have represented a "kind of death" for her, though we can infer, thinking back to "Octet," that the statement implies the death of some idea or "picture" of herself. Perhaps it was the picture of herself as a free agent to whom the life and needs of a psychotic rapist had absolutely no relevance. It is this kind of dependency—on the desires and even the whims of others—in any case, that the interviewee shows himself unable to accept in his own interaction with the interviewer, even as he insists on the supposedly transformational effect the woman's story had had on him.

It is also the willingness to risk this kind of death—the death of the imperious, free subject, able to think or talk itself to certainty—that for Wallace separates morally efficacious from merely self-serving rhetorical "nakedness." At the end of the interview, when the man claims to "stand naked" before the interviewer, we are invited to compare his nakedness with the woman's. But in drawing attention to his (figurative) nakedness, the interviewee has already registered a self-consciousness about nakedness that separates him inexorably from the woman. Moreover, that self-consciousness is accompanied by hostility, as is made more than apparent in the interview's explosive conclusion:

> "It didn't matter if she was fluffy or not terribly bright. Nothing else mattered. She had all my attention. I'd fallen in love with her. I believed she could save me. I know how this sounds, trust me. I know your type and I know what you're bound to ask. Ask it now. This is your chance. I felt she could save me I said. Ask me now. Say it. I stand here naked before you. Judge me, you chilly cunt. You dyke, you bitch, cooze, cunt, slut, gash. Happy now? All borne out? Be happy, I don't care. I knew she could. I knew I loved. End of story." (271)

In a book in which it can seem that, as Zadie Smith points out, the questions are "not only formally 'missing' from the conversation, [but] *their respondents have internalized them*,"[27] one might think that the *explosiveness* of the interviewee's anger would be underwritten by his own suspicion that his emotional conversion was in some sense fraudulent, self-serving, or narcissistic. But this accounts for only part of the man's anger. As throughout Wallace's book, what makes the man truly hideous is laid bare by his language, throughout the interview and here in its final moments—where he is fully revealed, nakedly as it were, though not in the manner he supposes. The verbs he uses to express his conviction that he had been saved, each one further down the road to certainty than the last ("I *believed* she could save me"; "I *felt* she could save me"; "I *knew* she could [save me]"), should remind us of the metaphysical and historical uncertainty that underlies the personal one throughout the collection ("One never knew . . . "). The interviewee is not content with believing he had been saved or even with feeling he could have been saved; he is only "borne out" when he arrives at certain knowledge. The violence of his language is provoked by his frustration that his words fail to *prove* to the female interviewer what he himself "knows." Though he continuously refers to the interviewer's skepticism—and by proxy his own self-doubt—he is incapable of accepting that words alone are incapable of (dis)solving that skepticism. If the rhetorical assault of the female interviewer can only be seen as approximating the physical one recounted by the woman inside the story, in both cases we see how the attacks represent not a failure of communication but the inability to recognize that communication cannot be rescued from the possibility of failure.

"B.I. #20" does not, as has sometimes been supposed, offer a program for future fiction—exemplified, say, by the woman's sincere delivery of her story. What we feel of the girl's "sacred otherness"[28] is a product of the hideous man's distance from her; even as we are attracted to the picture he draws of her, we cannot help but see it as a figment of his ambivalent romanticization. Indeed, even as he praises her "rhetorical innocence," he conveys something else—a hostility toward that innocence, combined with doubt about its authenticity and mirrored by his skepticism about his own authenticity. Moreover, in coming to see the rapist as literalizing his own tendencies toward women, the hideous man only *appears* to have made a "profound" breakthrough, for he shows from the words "let me explain" that he has not drawn the relevant lesson.

Like the rest of the men in the collection, the final interviewee has not learned how to bring his explanation to an end—or, say, that the "love" he professes in the opening sentence is not the kind of thing that can be certified via explanation. When Wittgenstein speaks of not being able to "get outside" of a picture, because the picture "lay in our language, and language seemed to repeat it to us inexorably" (*PI* §115), he was talking of this man, and to any aspects of his fantasy of independence that we may share with him. The hideous man had earlier analogized himself to the rapist because of his intention to leave the woman with a fake phone number; the real analogy, however, consists in his refusal to accept the independence of a female's judgment of him. The craving for certainty is thus revealed to be not just confused or selfish but, in this final case, truly monstrous—a fount of misogyny and violence both rhetorical and otherwise.

◆ ◆ ◆

"A perspicuous representation," writes Wittgenstein, "produces just that understanding which consists in 'seeing connections.'"[29] Reviewers and commentators on *Brief Interviews* have wanted to see the hideous men as either eccentric ("florid and exotic") representatives of our narcissistic culture or as redundant ones. But if we agree that the hideous men, like the interviewee in "B.I. #20," have mastered a way of speaking that is spread widely among educated elites of all sexes, and that the goal of the stories is to help us see connections between what we normally admire about such ways of speaking and what by the end of the collection we recognize as being truly hideous about the people who employ them, then it is hard to see how the stories could be either eccentric or redundant.

This does not mean that the therapies offered in the book are for everyone. But I hope that the discussion in this chapter has shown that the book has relevance even beyond its application to a specific brand of twenty-first-century intellectualized misogyny. Or, to put this another way, Wallace's collection locates this intellectualized misogyny within a horizon of beliefs and practices both literal and literary, many of which are far from limited to misogynists.

In an essay entitled "Beyond Philosophy: David Foster Wallace on Literature, Wittgenstein, and the Dangers of Theorizing," Randy Ramal suggests that Wallace shared with Wittgenstein a suspicion of philosophy's overreliance on theory, with both understanding "theoretical explanations to be too generalized and distorting of the phenomena they seek to explain."[30] I think that Wallace and Wittgenstein did share an insight about the "dangers of theorizing," but it is not the one Ramal identifies. There is nothing *dangerous* about a theoretical explanation that distorts or simplifies certain phenomena. This is simply a feature of theoretical explanations—theories explain some things well and other things less well; the principle of scientific progress is based on the idea that a new theory will account for more phenomena more accurately than the one before it. What Wittgenstein and Wallace saw as "dangerous" about theoretical explanation was rather the way it could become habitual, crowding out or demoting all other forms of justification. A whole culture could be captivated by theoretical explanation as simply *the* mode of sophisticated thinking and communication.

Wittgenstein believed in his time that something like this had happened to a certain group of academic philosophers; Wallace's insight is that, in our time, many of us even outside of academia have come to resemble such philosophers, refusing to acknowledge that there are modes of human interaction that theoretical explanation does as much to corrupt as to facilitate.

Far from being merely a psychological commentary on certain neuroses or eccentric prejudices, then, Wallace's collection targets a specific historical and philosophical predicament, one that accords an unrivaled prominence to theoretical explanation. The collection places its characters in situations—usually moral situations, involving the uncertainties the hideous men associate with other people and especially with women—such that we are able to see why to deal with a problem only on the level of theory is often not to deal with it at all; worse, it is to deceive oneself about whether one is dealing with it or not. Hence the connection between the final hideous man's promise to "explain" his love and his explosive anger when he feels he has failed to explain it. *His* problem with theoretical explanation is not that it distorts certain phenomena but that it has become a habit rather than a choice.

"Suppose that Descartes discovered for philosophy that to confront the threat of our temptation to skepticism is to risk madness," writes Cavell, going on to say that since the *Philosophical Investigations* confronts the "temptation" to skepticism at every point, it "finds its victory in never claiming a final philosophical victory over (the temptation to) skepticism, which would mean a victory over the human."[31] *Brief Interviews* presents many characters seeking to secure victory over skepticism and thereby over their dependence on other people and on the external world—a view from "forever overhead," as it were. In criticizing this aspiration—a criticism carried out not through analysis but via a representation of its practical and moral consequences—Wallace encourages just such an endless refusal of victory. This can sound irritating, and exhausting, words critics of the book have not hesitated to use in describing it. And no one reader can settle the question of whether the stories will be worth the trouble for another. But surely, the only way one can answer for oneself is to dive into them.

4

Untrendy Problems

The Pale King's
Philosophical Inspirations

It is not all books that are as dull as their readers. There are probably
words addressed to our condition, which, if we could really hear and
understand, would be more salutary than the morning or the spring to our
lives, and possibly put a new aspect on the face of things for us.

—Henry David Thoreau, "Walden"

EARLY IN WALLACE'S CAREER, nonacademic critics often chided
him for his "pretentious" postmodern difficulty, a criticism that
I have argued sprang from a confusion about the use of postmodern techniques in his fiction.[1] But in the years following his death,
a new and more instructive criticism of his writing emerged. This
criticism was expressed in different ways, by different kinds of critics. One symptom of it is apparent in Hubert Dreyfus and Sean Dorrance Kelly's chapter on Wallace in their book on modern ethics, *All
Things Shining* (2011). Dreyfus and Kelly begin by calling Wallace
"the greatest writer of his generation; perhaps the greatest mind altogether," yet in what follows they suggest that his ethical outlook
was juvenile and hubristic and can usefully be compared to that of

the memoirist Elizabeth Gilbert.[2] A second version, or variety, of this kind of criticism can be found in Jonathan Franzen's 2011 *New Yorker* essay, "Farther Away." Wallace, Franzen suggests, was a gifted writer with a rare talent for describing midwestern weather, whose fiction was marred by his penchant for "moralism and theologizing," bad habits at least partially attributable (Franzen implies) to his lifelong battle with mental illness.[3] A third instance appears in an article by the critic Gerald Howard, posted on Salon.com late in 2012. Howard, who helped edit Wallace's first novel, confesses disappointment with Wallace's late fiction and essays and especially with Wallace's famous Kenyon commencement speech, which struck him as "uncomfortably close to those books of affirmations, no doubt inspiring but of questionable use when the hard stuff arrives."[4]

What these three commentaries share, despite differences in tone and intention, is the identification of Wallace with a directness and earnestness about moral matters that is considered to be excessive and possibly jejune. All three critics express an anxiety, even an embarrassment, about the fact that Wallace, especially in his later fiction and essays, really did commit himself to "untrendy human problems and emotions," just as he had promised he would in his oft-quoted early essay on television and fiction, "E Unibus Pluram" (*SFT* 81). They express their condescension toward this commitment by implying, each in his own way, that it stems from fundamentally "personal" concerns rather than, say, literary or philosophical ones.[5]

I am less interested in defending Wallace against the charge that his later fiction and essays resemble "books of affirmations" than I am in showing how his late fiction therapeutically questions the assumption that motivates the charge—namely, that the genre to which such books belong, call it "self-help," operates in a region distinct from and irrelevant to what we take to be more serious forms of culture. One way to credit the "insights" above, without crediting their implication of reproach, would be to say that they indicate, far better than the charge that Wallace was an overclever postmodernist, that to take Wallace seriously as a thinker is to take seriously his fervent commitment to the problems of the self. But that does not mean that that commitment need be perceived as grossly personal, or sentimental, or that it should consign Wallace's writing to the same kind of (in)attention we reserve for what we normally call self-help literature. Indeed, one of the things Wallace's fiction demonstrates is how problems customarily cordoned off into self-help, or (in their high form) "psychology," are also philosophical problems or, at least, have components that can be best addressed philosophically.

The Pale King, long portions of which delve into themes from the Kenyon commencement, is the book critics have been most apt to associate with Wallace's supposed deviation into sentimentality, moralism, or self-help. And it is true that in *The Pale King* we find Wallace at his most morally direct. But it is no coincidence that we can also find in Wallace's late, unfinished novel some of the most vivid examples of the strategies he employed in the hopes of returning literature—and the people reading it—from the high ledge of abstraction and theory to the concrete conundrums of everyday experience.

Because Wallace's final published fiction was posthumously pieced together by his longtime editor Michael Pietsch, following the author's death in 2007, it would be foolish to assess it in the same way as Wallace's other works of fiction. For that reason I plan in this chapter to treat two parts of the book largely independently, as separable passages of writing that both illuminate and, in the second case, show the limits of what I have been calling Wallace's philosophically therapeutic project.

The first of those, the section of the novel dealing with the mental history of IRS auditor Meredith Rand, makes explicit a distinction that runs throughout Wallace's fiction, between the form of philosophical therapy he hoped his fiction would offer to his readers and the more conventional forms of therapy that characterize our "therapeutic age"[6]—and to which Wallace elsewhere subjects his characters. The second is the longest continuous portion of the book, dealing with the spiritual transformation of IRS auditor Chris Fogle. In that case I argue that Wallace fully indulges, perhaps for the first time in his *fiction*, his desire to move beyond the confines of negative therapy to full-fledged exhortation. Linking Fogle's "journey of ascent" in this section with

Cavell's idea of "perfectionism," I will ask whether such a move can be thought to extend Wittgenstein's philosophically therapeutic method or whether it should be considered a break from it.

REALLY LOOKING

If much of Wallace's mature fiction can be viewed fruitfully as a "series of examples" meant to treat the point of view he takes to be characteristic of his readership, the strategy is rarely as transparent as it is in *The Pale King*. Particularly, it can be seen at work in the series of dialogues recounted at a bar after work one night by the accountant Meredith Rand.

The story Rand tells revolves around several sessions with a sickly nighttime attendant at a recovery center where, as a teenager, she had been sent for "cutting." The attendant was not a doctor, Rand makes sure to point out, but rather a "natural therapist" who spoke to Rand as if he were "talking to a child"—that is, to "somebody so locked into the problem that she can't even see that it's her problem and not just the way the world is" (499). It is not immediately clear what Rand means by calling the attendant a "natural therapist," but the dialogues she recounts with him certainly resemble the "scenes of instruction" in Wittgenstein's *Philosophical Investigations*, in which a "central character is the child."[7] The late-night attendant, for instance, explained to Rand that she had set herself a "neat little trap [to] ensure that I never really had to grow up and so I could stay immature and waiting forever for somebody to save me" (498). The trap was common to women in Rand's extremely juvenile or adolescent generation, the attendant said. Rand's real wish was to be able to "go around thinking that my real problem was that no one could see or love the real me the way I needed so I'd always have my problem to sit and hold and stroke on and make believe was the real problem" (498).

We might be tempted to call the trap the attendant describes "psychological" rather than "philosophical." For Wallace, it does not matter what we call the trap; what matters is how we treat it. Psychology has its customary ways of treating it, and these ways of treating it, as Wallace goes on about *ad nauseam* in his fiction, are not likely to help Rand with her "core problem" and possibly not even with its symptoms (e.g., the cutting). The biggest difference between the attendant's therapy and the therapy practiced by the conventionally trained doctors at the facility is that the attendant informs Rand that "it doesn't ultimately matter why I do it or what it, like, represents. . . . All that matters is that I was doing it and to stop doing it." The doctors, however, "thought that diagnosis was the same as cure. That if you knew why, you would stop" (486). Rand calls this latter thought "bullshit," which is a succinct summary of Wallace's own judgment, in an early essay, of the "frankly idealistic" contemporary—postmodern, but also modern—belief that "etiology and diagnosis pointed toward cure, that a revelation of imprisonment led to freedom" (*SFT* 66). As I mentioned in my introduction, Wallace traces this "idealistic" belief as far back as Descartes, although it was Freud who claimed psychological benefits for those willing to apply Descartes's enlightenment rationalism to their own inner life. Wallace does adapt some of Freud's psychoanalytic insights into his form of writing, but his method is ultimately anti-Freudian in its ambivalence and even skepticism about the value of introspection, which Wallace emphasizes can become an addiction as destructive as any other. The sickly late-night attendant teaches Rand that "it doesn't matter why I cut or what the psychological machinery is behind the cutting, like if it's projecting self-hatred or whatever. Because whatever the institutional reason, it's hurting myself, it's me being mean to myself, which was childish" (*PK* 506).

Evidently, since it is repeated several times, this is a conclusion Wallace senses his reader will be apt to doubt or misinterpret. The attendant's point is not that institutions have nothing to do with Rand's problem (how could he know what they have to do with it? how could she?); it is that, at the pass she has come to, it will not help Rand to understand her problems as being produced by her upbringing or by the "structure" of her society, and that it is precisely this way of thinking that keeps her "going around and around inside" of her problem as opposed to "really looking" at it (496). But what does it mean to "really look" at one's problems? This is at the heart of the therapy that Wallace's proxy, the attendant, is offering. The more experienced doctors at Rand's clinic in this case represent our default cultural answer to the question: to "really look," they explain to Rand, is to investigate causes and symptoms analytically, just as Wallace's academic critics have so often encouraged *him* to do. But the attendant's visual framing of the problem—it is significant that he says "really look" as opposed to "really understand"—serves to reinforce the Wittgensteinian difference in Wallace's approach, the deepest target of which is Rand's adolescent—one might say "romantic"—philosophical picture of herself.

As in Wallace's short story "The Depressed Person," the dialogue here reproduces in spirit if not in exact wording certain moments from the section on private language in the *Philosophical Investigations*. "I wanted people to look past the prettiness thing and the sexual thing and see who I was, like as a person," Rand says, "and I felt really mad and sorry for myself that people didn't." But "in reality," the attendant gets her to see, "everything was the surface . . . because under the surface were just all these feelings and conflicts about the surface; about how I looked and the effect on people I had" (499). Rand, in other words, had concocted an unknowable private self, yet this private self held no content, for in fact what lay "under the surface" was only a constant worry about what other people were seeing on the surface. The problem is what Wittgenstein would call "grammatical." It requires not a theoretical unmasking—for there is nothing, Rand now sees, beneath the mask—but a therapy focused on the way Rand is using such concepts as "self" to frame her self-description. "Such an investigation," says Wittgenstein, "sheds light on our problem by clearing misunderstandings away. Misunderstandings concerning the use of words, caused, among other things, by certain analogies between the forms of expression in different regions of language."[8] In Rand's case, the lonely, private self is born and endlessly reproduced in phrases like the "real me" and "under the surface." The sickly attendant might have told Rand that "the human body is the best picture of the human soul."[9]

As is often the case when Wallace depicts a therapeutic process, the extent to which the sickly late-night attendant's message has really sunk in for Rand—the extent to which she now lives what she claims to have learned from him—is unclear and not just (I don't think) because Wallace never finished *The Pale King*. Rand tells the entire story about her time at the rehabilitation center to an IRS coworker, Shane Drinion, during an after-work happy hour. The conversation is punctuated by

Rand's anxiety that what she is saying is "boring" or "banal" (that her story is no more interesting, or deserving of respect, than self-help); moreover, as she gets deeper into the story, she begins to imitate aspects of her younger, less mature self (489). Drinion, described by coworkers as "possibly the dullest human being currently alive" (448), is nevertheless capable of exceptional feats of attention, so much so that he is later said to participate in an auditing competition with a computer. Toward the end of the story, having paid close attention to what Rand is telling him (not only is Drinion never bored; he claims not to know what the word means), Drinion wonders matter-of-factly at the paradox that, though the sickly attendant had seemed to teach Rand a valuable lesson about her childish and self-destructive need to be "saved," the story casts the attendant himself—who later became Rand's husband—as precisely the savior she had so childishly been looking for. Rand admits this paradox and cannot resolve it.

Insofar as Wallace's therapy is always aimed ultimately at his reader, it is fitting that his fiction's most explicit scene of therapeutic instruction would include a kind of warning about the inherent dangers in therapy—philosophical or otherwise—of idolatry. This may have been meant, in part, as a warning to some of his own, often idolatrous, readers. To the extent that critics have attempted to pierce the glow of "Saint Dave" by drawing attention to Wallace's problems with depression or addiction, or to his mistreatment of women, they show the logic behind Wallace's own discomfort with the idea that some may look to him for moral wisdom. Yet, as I have been arguing throughout this book, Wallace, in attempting to do something more than provide pleasure or beauty for his readers—in claiming his fiction was actually addressed to their sense of "lostness" or confusion—clearly contributed to his own sanctification, thereby putting himself in a position to be evaluated as a new parent for a readership he often imagined as wayward and adolescent.

A second, harder point of the scene—or of the indeterminacy of Rand's therapeutic outcome—might be described like this: there is no once-and-for-all way to escape, to put behind us for good, the human dimension of adolescence. One way to summarize Rand's problem as a teenager is to say that she was narcissistic; that is, she thought her difficulties were special rather than common or natural. This is an adolescent thought, but it is also a human one. The grammatical point would be that the problem was not with Rand's narcissism but with her perspective on her narcissism—namely, the perspective that made her narcissism into a bigger and different kind of problem ("just the way the world is") than it was.[10] But Wallace's fiction is not merely censorious of this attitude; it shows how seductive and even natural it is. Rand's conversations at the recovery center helped her to see her problem from a new vantage, but they did not offer—as most self-anointed self-helpers would—a permanent solution to it. If we equate such conversations with the kind Wallace attempted to carry on with his readers, then this would be one way of underscoring the interminability (and also the inexhaustibility) of Wallace's literary-philosophical project. The "series of examples" can go on and on; our need for "reminders" will come to an end only when life does.

At a climactic moment in the conversation between Rand and Drinion, much remarked on by reviewers of *The Pale King*, Drinion is said to be "levitating slightly"[11] as he becomes so "completely immersed" in Rand's story that he loses consciousness of himself (487). This is Wallace's way of dramatizing Drinion's complete innocence and impartiality—a kind of fantasy of unselfconsciousness that held no small appeal for many in Wallace's television-obsessed generation.[12] Yet Wallace seems to suggest, precisely with such notes as the levitation, that Drinion has not overcome narcissism; he has never felt it; hence he is not properly human, rather in- or sub- or superhuman. Nothing in the therapy Rand receives would put her on a path toward becoming Drinion, for Drinion has not mastered the problem of narcissism so much as he has been spared from it. (A similar point could be made with regard to the relationship between Hal and his deformed brother Mario in *Infinite Jest*.) At the same time, one can sense the appeal of such a figure for Wallace, and long portions of *The Pale King* explore how a more normally self-conscious being might approximate Drinion's mystical equanimity and focus. The most prominent of these sections is the one recounting the story of Chris Fogle.

BEING SERIOUS

Like Wallace's fiction, significant portions of Stanley Cavell's philosophy grapple with the question of how to inherit the late Wittgenstein.

"Moral Perfectionism" combined for Cavell the instructive or therapeutic elements he admired in the *Philosophical Investigations* with
more traditional modes of literary-philosophical "inspiration," evident in works as diverse as Augustine's *Confessions*, Kierkegaard's *Ei-
ther/Or*, and Emerson's "Experience." In the introduction to his Carus
Lectures Cavell describes perfectionism as a long but oft-neglected
tradition in Western thought concerned with "what used to be called
the state of one's soul," and he imagines philosophy less as a search for
better facts than as a "journey of ascent" toward a better self.[13] In lieu
of further definition, he advances a list of texts containing perfectionist elements, beginning with Plato's *Republic* and Shakespeare's *Hamlet*
and carrying on to his own "doorstep" with works by Freud, Thoreau,
Beckett, and Wittgenstein.

Even more than Rand, Chris Fogle is imagined, in the longest continuous portion of *The Pale King*, as the product of an extended and
debilitating adolescence. But the pivotal sequence in Fogle's life involves
not a set of therapeutic conversations but a lecture, almost a sermon,
that presents as inspirational precisely what Fogle, in his conformity
with his culture, had previously viewed as banal or pathetic. This is what
marks the section, for me, as being more perfectionist than philosophically therapeutic. In tone and method it resembles less the Wittgenstein
of *Philosophical Investigations* than it does the Kierkegaard of *Either/Or*
or the Thoreau of "Walden." For Cavell, such texts were precursors for
a project he initially identified with Wittgenstein. After describing how
The Pale King can be read as participating in the perfectionist tradition,
I will register some doubt as to whether the core perfectionist works
mentioned by Cavell—inherited by Wallace in this section—really can
be fit into the Wittgensteinian therapeutic project.

Perfectionism arises out of the intuition that life can stop being meaningful to us or that we act in such a way that the meaning is drained out
of it and therefore fail to live up to our best or higher selves, the selves
we are, as Emerson says, when we "best know" who we are.[14] The great
philosophical enemy of the perfectionist text is therefore skepticism or
nihilism—intimately related in Cavell's hands—but with these words
being understood to describe less a self-conscious philosophical position
than a perspective or a way of life. In the course of his narration Chris

Fogle refers to his younger self as a nihilist no less than four times, but he does not mean by this that he aspired to live according to the dictates of Nietzsche or Schopenhauer. Fogle's nihilism, rather, was the result of what he unreflectively assimilated from his culture and upbringing. Like many in his generation, Fogle says, he "was not raised as anything" and as a teenager he romanticized what he now recognizes as a "narcissistic despair" (166). (He might have said that he and his friends felt a "stereotyped but unconscious despair.")[15] It wasn't until sixth grade that Fogle learned the definition of the word *nihilism*—appropriately, in the "sixth week of theater class in high school" (163)—by which time he was already on his way to becoming "a real nihilist," who "drifted and quit because nothing meant anything, no one choice was really better" (223). In this he was much like his peers. "Everyone I knew and hung out with was a wastoid," he remembers. "It was hip to be ashamed of it, in a strange way . . . or just to feel directionless and lost" (165).

Several events, including the untimely death of his father in a gruesome subway accident, prepared Fogle for what he describes as his "change in direction"—that is, his move out of or beyond nihilism. But Fogle did not finally manage to "put away childish things" (172) until he wandered, mistakenly, into an advanced accounting class at the Catholic DePaul University in Chicago. The class was being taught by a "substitute Jesuit"—in a Freudian slip, Fogle later calls him a "substitute father" (176)—capable of summarizing extant property tax law with a dry yet apparently undeniable majesty. At the end of the class, in what is alternately a parody and a paraphrase of Kierkegaard, the Jesuit delivers a peroration on the necessity of the "leap outward" into adulthood. The leap is into "reality," where there is "no audience," but from the perspective of which all other kinds of heroism appear as mere "theater" (229). The students in the class had so far lived a "crude approximation of a human life," the Jesuit says. Real heroism or courage was not what they thought it was. To work day after day at a thankless job, giving oneself to "the care of other people's money"—this was "effacement, perdurance, sacrifice, . . . valor" (231).

For all its hyperbole, the speech works a change in Fogle. The change begins with his recognition that he had so far been living a *"crude approximation of a human life"* (237, italics in original). The recognition

is inseparable from his realization that there might be something else
he could be living—for example, what Thoreau called a "whole human
life."[16] As Cavell points out, perfectionist thinkers do not take sides in the
various Kantian problematics that occupy much of professional moral
philosophy; their concern is not with what *should* compel us to change
our behavior but with what *does*. By showing us visions of our rejected
selves, of selves that look better than our current ones, such texts hope
to trigger in us "that aversion to ourselves in our conformity that will
constitute our becoming, as it were, ashamed of our shame."[17] For Fogle,
the Jesuit functions something like a substitute self, manifesting exactly
the qualities that Fogle believed he had rejected in himself: the Jesuit "was
'indifferent'—not in a meaningless, drifting, nihilistic way, but rather
in a secure, self-confident way"; he had "a kind of zealous integrity that
manifested not as style but as the lack of it"; he didn't feel the need to
"joke or try to slightly undercut what he was about to say" (226).

Here is a virtual catalogue of the qualities Wallace himself said he
admired in certain literary "authorities," such as Dostoyevsky, but that
he confessed were difficult to reproduce, both for himself personally
and for any contemporary writer, in a cultural climate where the undermining of authority was valued more highly than the expression
of it. This is one reason for taking the Fogle section, despite its own
undercutting gestures—in a certain mood the substitute Jesuit can
seem merely hilarious, and it is hinted that Fogle's "transformation"
was at least in part abetted by a prescription drug—as the moral and
philosophical center of *The Pale King*, the place where readers become
averse to their own penchant for "hip nihilism" and the romanticization of despair. Fogle, for his part, now sees that all his own "nonconformist" behavior was little more than theater: "I remember once
shaving off just one sideburn and going around like that for a period
of time, believing the one sideburn made me a nonconformist—I'm
not kidding" (161). Later he announces the discovery of a better,
deeper self:

> There were depths in me that were not bullshit or childish but pro-
> found, and were not abstract but much realer than my clothes or self-
> image, and that blazed in an almost sacred way—I'm being serious;
> I'm not just trying to make it more dramatic than it was. (189)

That this is one of the places Fogle stops to insist ("I'm being *serious* . . . ") hints at what Wallace takes to be the radicality of the claim, for his audience, that there might be something "much realer" than one's personality. The idea, though, that there is a self that lies deeper than the ego is a relatively familiar one from transcendental philosophy to the teachings of the Eastern mystics. Perhaps what is most radical, or challenging, about the story is the fact that Fogle believes his access to those inner depths has something to do with his decision to work as an accountant for the IRS.

American fiction has generally privileged characters who have preferred not to assent to the deadening daily grind of office work, and popular culture boasts no shortage of books and TV shows whose comedy is predicated on the widespread consensus that the white-collar office is as absurd and soul-destroying as it is inescapable.[18] Among academics, too, actually existing social institutions are not often held up as models of liberatory potential. Wallace's contrasting attitude toward institutions like the IRS is another clue to how far the approximations of him as a nihilistic postmodernist missed their mark. As with the more recent criticism from nonacademic critics that I mentioned earlier, the academic critics have caught up in this regard. In "The Institution of Nothing: David Foster Wallace in the Program," Mark McGurl criticizes Wallace for what he calls his "existentialism of institutions"—his tendency, that is, to equate "getting with the program" with liberation. "Whether it is a nursing home, a halfway house, Alcoholics Anonymous, a tennis academy, mammoth federal bureaucracy, or the university," writes McGurl, "the 'institution' in Wallace is first and foremost a communal antidote to atomism, a laboriously iterated wall against the nihilism attendant to solitude."[19]

McGurl's essay is helpful in pointing out one of the distinctive facets of Wallace's fiction: his belief that some institutions that intellectuals and artists tend to look down on might hold genuine transformational potential. In a footnote to this very passage, however, McGurl concedes a point that would seem to complicate, if not undermine completely, his argument that Wallace is naively affirmative toward such institutions. McGurl notes that Wallace distinguishes between different institutions according to their "social ends."[20] The IRS processing center in *The Pale King* and

Ennet House in *Infinite Jest*, McGurl acknowledges, do not play the same role in their respective books as do the MFA program in "Westward the Course of Empire Takes Its Way" and Enfield Tennis Academy in *Infinite Jest*. The tennis academy and the MFA program both fail spectacularly to provide their individual members with a stable sense of meaning—or, so to speak, with any relief from their fear and loathing of Bad Things. Wallace makes clear that they fail because, as institutions, they tend to reinforce regnant capitalistic values like individualism and competition alongside broader cultural dominants such as cleverness, irony and the conflation of intelligence with a facility for abstract reasoning. These are precisely the cultural values that are called into question by Alcoholics Anonymous as it is portrayed in *Infinite Jest* and then again by the IRS processing center that is the main setting of *The Pale King*.

Indeed, the effectiveness of *The Pale King*, or of its philosophical instruction, may depend on the reader coming to see that the renunciation of conformism can take many forms and that the forms of rebellion we learned about as adolescents will likely turn out to have been adolescent. Even the tax collector could escape conformism, said Kierkegaard, because conformism was a matter of inner freedom and not, as we may be tempted to believe in our eternal adolescence, a matter of "self-image." The moral lesson of Fogle's monologue is intrinsic to his recognition that his choice to work for the IRS, which had looked to the younger Fogle like it would represent a narrowing of his freedom, led instead to the discovery of a "much realer" self than the one that had "chosen to have nothing matter." The monologue thus doubles as a demonstration of the point Wallace emphasizes somewhat more dramatically in his Kenyon commencement—that even the "tedious and the dronelike" can be understood, if we really *choose* it, "as not only meaningful, but sacred, on fire with the same force that made the stars."[21]

BEYOND THERAPY

A difference between Rand's and Fogle's philosophical journeys might be described as follows: whereas Rand is brought, via a series of interactive dialogues, to see the contingency of what she had been convinced was her real self ("the real me"), Fogle is inspired, primarily by the Jesuit's peroration, to trade a false or a shallow for a real or a deep self. In a sense, then, Fogle ends up where Rand begins. In another sense Fogle progresses to a state that is unimagined by (the teenage *or* the adult) Rand—call it authenticity, or wholeness, or happiness, or grace.

The fact that Rand would be unable to imagine it, however, may prompt us to question how Wallace's own conception of such a state reflects back on his predominantly negative therapeutic project. The difficulty—bordering on the impossibility—of narratively dramatizing such states of grace is one of the explicit topics of other portions of *The Pale King*;[22] moreover, it may be responsible for what Wallace came to see as the almost insurmountable challenge of completing the book.[23] For the purposes of this chapter, it is also relevant that the aspiration to positively imagine such a condition may tip aspects of the book into the very kind of sentimental moralism that Wallace tried so hard elsewhere to avoid.

Cavell implies that perfectionism is an outgrowth of Wittgenstein's notion of philosophy as therapy,[24] as if the goal of philosophical therapy is the same kind of grace that is vouchsafed to the Kierkegaardian knight of faith. But the difference between Rand's and Fogle's stories in *The Pale King* demonstrates a consequential distinction between their methods of instruction or inspiration. Famously, Wittgenstein maintained that the philosopher should not speak directly about ethics. In contrast to many of the authors Cavell counts as perfectionist, he does not offer his reader a vision of some better, more authentic or more awake way of living; he does not speak at all (as Thoreau does) of a "*whole* human life," or of an ethically or spiritually fulfilling life (as Kierkegaard or Augustine might), or of an authentic or a natural one (as do Heidegger and Rousseau). Wittgenstein speaks strictly of a human life, and of the human being's all-too-human desire to go beyond the human, and thus of her need constantly to be called back to herself or to her humanity—a condition he calls "peace," which is always temporary.[25]

Rand's therapeutic progress in *The Pale King* remains provisional; and, for his part, the "sickly" late-night attendant is not presented as leading a spiritually superior life to Rand's, only a (slightly) less tortured one. In Fogle's section, however, there is a suggestion that certain lives are not just more peaceful than others but that they may be lived at a higher, or deeper, or more sacred pitch. In the notes arranged after the culmination of *The Pale King*'s narrative, probably the most quoted passage in reviews of the book, there lies a vision of a life lived in what might be called the sacramental key:

> It turns out that bliss—a second-by-second joy + gratitude at the gift of being alive, conscious—lies on the other side of crushing, crushing boredom. Pay close attention to the most tedious thing you can find (tax returns, televised golf), and, in waves, a boredom like you've never known will wash over you and just about kill you. Ride these out, and it's like stepping from black and white into color. Like water after days in the desert. (548)

We do not know how Wallace would have incorporated this passage into his novel—it appears in the notes next to other notations regarding Drinion—had he finished it. At the same time, the interest it has held for critics indicates that it encapsulates something that was new, or newly direct, about *The Pale King*. For all his desire to be a "morally passionate, passionately moral" writer in the Dostoyevskian mode (*CtL* 274), Wallace would seem to have accepted, in the majority of his mature fiction—possibly for different reasons, possibly not[26]—Wittgenstein's prohibition against direct ethical appeals. *The Pale King* marked a new stage in Wallace's development insofar as it aimed not merely to free his readers from philosophical confusion but also to galvanize them with a quasi-ascetic vision of a life ecstatically lived. If Rand's section reprises Wallace's attempt to give his readers some temporary "peace" from their torments, in Fogle's portion, and elsewhere in the book, there emerges a vision of a mode of experience that transcends the therapeutic, together with the "untrendy human troubles" it is meant to address, altogether.

If these can be described as the most perfectionist moments in the book, they are also connected intimately to *The Pale King*'s expression of the counterpart to perfectionism's lofty idealism—namely, its intense despair about our *present* condition. Cavell begins his lectures on perfectionism with the question of whether Moral Perfectionism is "inherently elitist" with regard to society, granting that "some idea of being true to oneself—or to the humanity in oneself, or of the soul as on a journey (upward or onward) . . . requires a refusal of society, perhaps above all of democratic, leveling society." Cavell argues that perfectionism, in fact, "happily consents to democracy" and is even inextricable from the "democratic aspiration" (1). Without evaluating Cavell's case for perfectionism as a democratic necessity, I want to raise the possibility that the consequences of perfectionism's elitism can manifest themselves personally—as elitism toward the unimproved self—even before they do so socially or politically, as elitism toward society as it stands. The sense that is voiced repeatedly by Thoreau at the beginning of "Walden"—that Americans are living impoverished or desperate lives, that they "labor under a mistake," that they are "doing penance in a thousand remarkable ways"[27]—finds its counterpart in the portions of *The Pale King* that regard its characters' self-consciousness and narcissism as symptoms of spiritual deficiency and cultural decline. When the critic Jonathan Raban described a "fundamentalist streak" in Wallace's final novel, it was likely these elements of the book's tone and subject matter that he had in mind.[28]

Doubtless Cavell would describe any "fundamentalism" in the book as marking a deviation from perfectionism, not an expression of it. Yet for the person who accepts Fogle's picture of the sacred within the human—which is also often perfectionism's picture—it may be hard to resist the conclusion that he is falling short of his highest, most authentic potential, failing to measure up to his "genius" (in Emerson's version) or to be who he is (in Nietzsche's). His sense of failure, of falling short of authenticity, or sincerity, is the engine that gets perfectionism going; the danger is just that, *therapeutically* speaking, that same sense of failure is also one of perfectionism's most likely outcomes.

The novel's aesthetic failure—its failure as a work of narrative drama—can also be connected to Wallace's ambition to artistically dramatize not just the ascent out of moral nihilism that characterizes perfectionism but, in some cases, the actual achievement of moral or spiritual maturity. In Kierkegaard's *Either/Or*, a book devoted to delineating the virtues of maturity against those of what might be called adolescence, the husband who writes the second letter affirms that the "ideal husband . . . cannot be represented" by art. This is because while poetry and art are made to represent things in the "process of becoming," the virtues of such a husband—humility, patience, consistency—are properly achieved only insofar as they are "present constantly."[29] *The Pale King* is not about marriage, but Fogle's internal reckoning with his younger self can be usefully compared to the dialogue in *Either/Or* between the seducer and the husband. The conflict is between what the substitute Jesuit implies are the juvenile or theatrical virtues of adolescence and the more mature virtues toward which Wallace had been attempting to guide his readers at least since the Alcoholics Anonymous portions of *Infinite Jest*. If *The Pale King* remains on firm and familiar ground in seeking to therapeutically expose the shortcomings of the adolescent outlook, the book's failure to cohere as a whole may be attributable, among other things, to Wallace's desire to go further than that, into the very territory that Kierkegaard had warned should be considered off-limits to dramatic art, since it could only be demonstrated, over long and painstaking duration, in life.

The book, moreover—precisely because it endeavors to move beyond the discourse of therapy—reflects, more than any of Wallace's other fiction, the problem for the secular intellectual who sees very well the insufficiency of the adolescent faith in unfettered personal freedom yet finds it difficult to articulate a rationale for any specific constraints or limitations on that freedom. Kierkegaard may have thought it impossible to dramatize the ethical life, but such a life undoubtedly had substantive content for him, supplied by Christianity. If we are finally given a glimpse, in *The Pale King*, of what lies in the "depths" that Don Gately glimpses during some of his AA sessions in *Infinite Jest*, what we see there is curiously empty. The form of "commitment" valorized in Wallace's final novel is essentially a commitment to being an uncomplaining adult, who suffers the indignities of life without making too much of them.

We should not belittle such an achievement: perhaps in a secular, pluralistic age, it is the best that can be hoped for. Still, looking back on Wallace's writing from a very different political and social moment, it seems likely that the modesty of his aspirations was related to his time in history. Shadowed by Fukuyama's "end of history," his was a generation for whom, as Lee Konstantinou has put it, "capitalism's Cold War victory, individual irony, and philosophical antifoundationalism [had] merged into a single discourse."[30] Konstantinou's argument that

Wallace responded to this predicament by valorizing the figure of "the believer"—in the image of the nonfiction magazine founded by Dave Eggers, Heidi Julavits, and Vendela Vida—offers, in my view, an insufficient account of the role played by therapeutic self-knowledge in Wallace's fiction. But Wallace's final novel does reveal some of the costs of his reluctance to endorse a specific social, political, or spiritual project to go alongside his therapeutic one.

◆ ◆ ◆

Having marked out why I take Wallace's final book to have been less effective than his previous mature fiction, I want to end this chapter by emphasizing two things that unite Rand's and Fogle's stories and that indicate something of the continuing relevance of Wallace's project for us today. The first has been the topic of much of this book: Wallace's preoccupation with self-knowledge and the modes and methods by which it might be achieved. The second, which I will expand on below, is the conjoining of states of philosophical confusion with stages of personal development—with childhood or adolescence—as if these are not simply biological moments we will grow out of but perennial human possibilities and temptations.

In regard to this second point I want again to emphasize the language that Rand and Fogle use to describe their younger selves. Rand was not just confused and self-indulgent; she was "going around and around inside the problem instead of really looking at the problem" (496). Fogle was not only dejected and aimless; he was "the worst kind of nihilist—the kind who didn't even know he was a nihilist" (154). In both cases the subject had assumed a philosophical position but without meaning to and without—until much later—recognizing that she or he had assumed one. Rand and Fogle thus both demonstrate how one can "go around and around" in a philosophical problem while all the time thinking that one is addressing it or—even more troubling—that there is nothing to be addressed. (It is precisely this ignorance that is "worst" about being a nihilist without knowing it.) This is why they furnish such clear-cut examples of Wallace's attempt to dramatize how philosophical problems manifest themselves in personal lives—even and especially in the personal lives of *non*philosophers.

A critic may maintain, perhaps condescendingly, that adolescence is a trivial and banal subject, surely a serious obstacle for certain damaged Americans like Rand and Fogle, and even something that may once have occupied a class of philosophers and poets (call them romantics) but, for all that, not particularly worthy of serious investigation today, when we have so many more pressing problems (McGurl recommends focusing on debt). A task worthy of Wallace criticism would be to make clear how Wallace shows adolescence to be not only *a* philosophical problem but to be *our* philosophical problem. This would be at the same time to show that there could be *no* words "addressed to our condition" that were not addressed to our—extended and debilitating—adolescence.

For *The Pale King*, like Thoreau's "Walden," posits that a whole culture can persist in a state of immaturity and blindness to itself. Possibly this culture fetishizes the notion of choice at the same time that it "chooses [like Chris Fogle] to have nothing matter" (223). In *The Pale King's* various "civics" chapters an argument hums about the truly awe-inspiring childishness of the American people, a people so sheltered and self-deluding that they could demand lower taxes and more public services at the same time and not even acknowledge the contradiction. They are "[not] infantile so much as adolescent," one of the accountants says of this benighted people, "that is, ambivalent about [their] twin desire for both authoritarian structure and the end of parental hegemony" (147).

In such an America the pervasiveness of self-help—not to mention books of affirmations, yoga, evangelical preaching, and television makeover shows—might be seen as evidence not of the insignificance or shallowness of the problem of adolescence but of its depth and profundity. A benefit of Cavell's coining of "Moral Perfectionism" is to remind us of, and give us a vocabulary for talking about, philosophy's perennial commitment to such a problem. The perfectionist, says Cavell, treats "what we call adolescence" less as a "phase of individual development [than as] a dimension of human existence as such."[31] It is simultaneously the dimension in us that desires to be helped but does not know what help it needs, that wants to change but is stuck within a perspective from which there appears to be no path forward or—more likely in what Wallace once called our national "confusion of permissions" (*IJ* 320)—so many paths forward that it seems impossible to ever choose one.

The ability of this self to transform itself is for the perfectionist hardly peripheral to philosophy; it is rather something like philosophy's guiding ambition, though one from which it is habitually distracted. To remain faithful to it may demand, among other things, an embrace of formal experimentation, as well as the courage to cross disciplinary boundaries into areas more usually reserved for literature, or religion, or therapy, even if that means risking one's thought being confused with what Cavell calls "debased perfectionisms"[32]—those omnipresent lists of instructions attempting to tell the self, as from the outside, and dogmatically, how it ought to improve. And perhaps this is the real problem with most self-proclaimed self-help: not that it is so often unhelpful (what would be the harm in that?) but that it can so easily become programmatic, even dangerous in its self-certainty.

The virtue of philosophy as perfectionism, or as therapy, would then lie in its ability to answer the question of how reading (or culture) may benefit the self without tyrannizing or sentimentalizing it. If *The Pale King* demonstrates the potential pitfalls of this approach, itself devolving at times into moralism or didacticism, at its best it still participates in a tradition of literature that does not offer answers so much as it prompts or "primes"[33] its readers to ask themselves certain kinds of questions.

The Pale King's narrative threads almost all coalesce into stories of conversion or transformation, with its narrators recounting their paths from a self-incurred immaturity to something resembling enlightenment, maturity, or wisdom. That maturity *requires* wisdom, or enlightenment —rather than just natural growth or experience—may be described as the discovery that unites Rand's and Fogle's narratives, just as it constitutes a recurring motif in philosophy from Plato to Kierkegaard to Wittgenstein to Cavell. The reader may ignore or condescend to such a discovery, but, if the Wallace of *The Pale King* is to be believed, such tactics will only postpone the inevitability of contending with it.

Conclusion

In Heaven and Earth

ALTHOUGH THIS BOOK is first and foremost a study of David Foster Wallace's fiction, it is also meant to be an experiment in seeing how philosophy and literature can work together. I've found promising models for doing this in the work of Iris Murdoch, Stanley Cavell, Cora Diamond, Martha Nussbaum, Richard Rorty, Toril Moi, and Robert Pippin, among others. In one way or another these scholars have all attempted to reproduce or excavate the thinking behind imaginative narrative works without reducing them to a disguised form of argumentative philosophy. Specifically, these authors have conceived of distinctive ways for literature to contribute to our self-knowledge or social consciousness—that is, for it to tell us things we do not already know from philosophy and possibly could not know were we to limit ourselves to philosophy's customary methods and tools.

Wallace represents a rewarding subject for this sort of approach, and I have even suggested that the unity, depth, and ongoing relevance of his project are hard to appreciate without it. But rather than summarizing my argument about the philosophically therapeutic method and aspiration of Wallace's fiction, I want to conclude by questioning an assumption that I made when I began studying Wallace's fiction.

To adequately treat the topics I raise here would require a whole other book, probably focused on a different kind of writer. Still, in the spirit of therapeutic self-examination, I hope it will be worthwhile to raise the question, even if briefly, of whether there really exists an "intersection" where literature and philosophy can be said to engage in a complementary activity.

♦ ♦ ♦

In his work on perfectionism Stanley Cavell groups together works of literature and philosophy according to his intuition that they both seek to engage their audience in a "journey of ascent."[1] Two of the books he includes in his attempt to describe perfectionism are Plato's *Republic* and Shakespeare's *Hamlet*.[2] If Plato's *Republic* is the canonical site of philosophy's exclusion of literature, it might be argued that the countervailing exclusion occurs in act 1 of *Hamlet*, when, after seeing the ghost of his dead father, Hamlet tells Horatio, "There are more things in heaven and earth . . . / Than are dreamt of in your philosophy."[3]

Given that these two archetypal works of Western culture virtually take as their point of departure an explicit exclusion of the other—that is, of art in Plato's case and of philosophy in Shakespeare's—it is worth asking how convincing Cavell's case is for assimilating them to a common project. I take the answer to be relevant to the question of if, or how, Cavell responds to his own earlier question, in *The Claim of Reason*, about whether philosophy can "know itself" once it allows art back into its just city.

In pointing out the affinity of Wallace's negative therapeutic project with Wittgenstein's, I have suggested a fundamental continuity between what Wittgenstein was aiming at in the *Philosophical Investigations* and what Wallace was hoping to achieve in such works as *Infinite Jest* and *Brief Interviews with Hideous Men*. To acknowledge this continuity is to acknowledge that the question of whether Wallace would be allowed into Plato's philosophical republic cannot be separated from the question of whether Wittgenstein would be allowed in. (Just to make sure my cards are on the table: I think they would both be allowed in.) But while I do not claim Wallace was unique in his aspiration to use literary means for philosophical ends, I also do not wish to imply that everyone we recognize as a great artist is actually a philosopher in disguise. In fact, thinking of artists like Wallace—or Tolstoy, or the contemporary filmmaker Terrence Malick—in the way I've outlined here may help reveal a deep but often unexamined fault line among "image-makers," between those who are fundamentally devoted to using images for philosophical ends and those who appear to be doing something else with them.

What is this "something else"? In book 10 of the *Republic* Plato indicates that the most consequential difference between art and philosophy is not a formal one—that is, that art uses images and philosophy reasoned argument or dialectic. Rather, the deeper difference between them is teleological. Whereas philosophy aims to lead its adherents out of the cave of ignorance and into the true light of the good, poetry and art are content to leave their audience "in the dark" (so to speak): not only do artists communicate with images, but they do not acknowledge any realm of truth that exists beyond them. It is precisely because of art's ability to make flickering shadows seem so much more interesting and appealing than they really are—viewed in the true light of philosophy—that artists must be banished from the philosophical republic.[4]

The typical response to this challenge, by philosophers who wish to save art for philosophy (e.g., Aristotle, Arendt, or Heidegger), and by artists who manifest philosophical ambitions (e.g., Tolstoy, Mann, or Wallace), has been to insist that art can lead its adherents toward the good, just as philosophy does, but via an alternative route—say, by educating unruly emotions or helping us to "purge" ourselves of them. Literature professors today who endeavor to show how fiction can benefit our political or social lives are likewise engaged in a project that hinges on coming up with a satisfying response to Plato's challenge. This means they accept the underlying premise of that challenge, which is that artists, *un*like philosophers, do not possess a characteristic subject matter or sphere of authority.

It is this premise that Shakespeare challenges in the passage I mentioned above. Horatio, a philosophy student who is visiting from Wittenberg, describes his and Hamlet's encounter with the ghost as "wondrous strange." "And therefore as stranger give it welcome," Hamlet responds, for "There are more things in heaven and earth, Horatio, / Than are dreamt of in your philosophy."[5]

Hamlet is talking specifically about the ghost, but the line can be read as making a larger claim, about the "more" that would always remain "strange" to philosophy yet is central to both the subject matter and the perspective of the arts. This "more" includes aspects of human experience like love, family, dreams, ghosts, sensuality, and the grief that attaches itself to the melancholy prince like a shadow. It is no accident that Plato sought to discipline or purge all of these things in the *Republic*; indeed, it can be argued that Plato's return to the poets in book 10 signals the extent to which the entire dialogue may be read as a contest not just with poets but with the aspects of human experience—family, sexual desire, grief, the fascination with death and decay—that feed the poetic imagination. The *Republic* is not only incidentally opposed to the "more" of art; it is *organized* to exclude it.

Hamlet is often referred to as a philosophical or a political drama, and many philosophers—Hegel, Freud, and Cavell among them—have attempted to show how the play can be read as directing its audience toward philosophical ends. As I have mentioned, Cavell conceives of Shakespeare as working in the perfectionist tradition—a tradition he believes spans the distance usually posited between philosophers and artists, showing both to be engaged in an activity whose most powerful image is Plato's allegory of the cave. But by emphasizing Hamlet's "more," I mean to cast doubt on the suggestion that we could or should span that distance in the way that Cavell recommends. This is not to say there can never be any benefit to reading Shakespeare's tragedies philosophically, as Cavell has often done. But it does mean that the philosophical critic, in accepting Plato's framework regarding the direction (up, out of the cave) and ultimate ambition (happiness, justice, or flourishing) of worthwhile thinking, has committed herself to reading a work of tragic art on terms other than those it might set for itself. It means that she begins by asking, as Cavell often does in his writing on Shakespeare, "What is the good of such a tragedy?"[6]

In the case of *Hamlet* Cavell answers thus: the play, he says, is about the "work of mourning." Paraphrasing the psychoanalyst Melanie Klein, he describes such work as being characterized by "the severing of investment, the detaching of one's interests, strand by strand, memory by memory, from their binding with an object that has passed, burying the dead." But, Cavell adds—rather conspicuously, considering the play under discussion—"the condition of this work is that you *want* to live."[7] *Hamlet*, his reading tells us, shows us how to live through our grief. But does it? This is the point where Cavell himself seems not to have considered a possibility that would appear obvious to anyone who has not already decided there is a philosophically recognizable "good" to *Hamlet*: that Hamlet, the character, may *not* want to live and that Shakespeare, his creator, may not think he *ought* to want to.

This is not the place for a full reading of *Hamlet* or of Cavell's interpretation of it. But I do want to briefly summarize an interpretation that I find more faithful to the play's spirit than Cavell's, one that emphatically rejects the notion of *Hamlet* as offering a therapeutic benefit of any kind. In Harold Bloom's reading, an expansion of Nietzsche's, it is not Hamlet's grief but his "insight into the horrible truth" about the world that forestalls him from taking action. Bloom emphasizes that if Shakespeare had wanted to help purge us of our grief, he chose a very strange ambassador to show us the way. The prince's melancholy may appear partial and extreme in act 1, but the mature Hamlet of act 5 does not so much overcome that grief as he learns to generalize it; the way Bloom puts it is that the Hamlet of act 5 has grown "sorrier for mankind than he is for himself."[8] If Socrates may be thought of as the Western exemplar of philosophical optimism—the view according to which death is a small thing, not even worth our fear—then Hamlet would seem to remind us of our ceaseless attraction, noted also by Freud, to our own annihilation.

This might seem a strange point to make at the end of a book that argues for a philosophically therapeutic literary criticism. For me, though, it is helpful in distinguishing which works are appropriate for this form of criticism and which will be more rewarding of a different kind of engagement. Wallace's greatest work of fiction, *Infinite Jest*, begins with a protagonist, Hal, whose blend of brilliance and existential angst recalls that of the Danish prince. But it is precisely the undermining of Hal's authority, and even of our interest in him as readers as the novel unfolds, that marks *Infinite Jest* as a work disciplined by philosophical ambition in the Platonic sense. I think it a worthwhile question to ask what the "good" is of *Infinite Jest*. I am less sure than I once was that such a question can be profitably asked of *Hamlet*, a play that seems to progressively deepen and confirm the authority and attractiveness of its protagonist's "pragmatic nihilism," as Bloom calls it.[9]

Therapy, philosophical or otherwise, depends not only on the idea that we want to live but also that we want some of the things that philosophers have always held to inhere in the good life: happiness, justice, maturity, peace. Plato's rhetorical achievement in the *Republic* and elsewhere is to make it seem that if tragic poets do not accept that this is what people want, it is because they are separated from true knowledge, live in confusion, or "keep company" with the lower, irrational parts of the soul. I think Wallace operates according to this logic in his fiction: it is why he seeks to show through his characters that what we often perceive as an existential lack is in fact attributable to a philosophical error. To see this is to see what is of most value about Wallace as a thinker. At the same time, it is to recognize the limitations of this value from a point of view that we might call the poetic. For it may be reasonable—if risky—to presume, based on what we now know of his life and death, that Wallace chose not to convey everything that he knew in his fiction: for instance, that there are things on heaven and earth we want even more than we want happiness.

Acknowledgments

Books are not quite like films, but they are collaborative projects in many more ways than we commonly admit—and this particular book would not have happened without the support of many mentors, friends, and family. I'd especially like to express my gratitude to Stuart Burrows, Harriet Cholden, Irad Kimhi, Joan Pippin, Robert Pippin, Marie Stone, Arnold Weinstein, and David Wellbery, all of whom have played a part in helping me learn how to read, write, and think about literature.

I'd also like to thank Timothy Aubry, Emily-Jane Cohen, Ben Jeffery, Paul Kottman, Jonny Thakkar, Rachel Wiseman, Etay Zwick, and again Robert Pippin for their crucial feedback and guidance on this project. A special thanks to my friend Kevin Simmons, who told me to read *Infinite Jest* when we were in high school—a recommendation it took me about five years to follow—and to Douglas Seibold, my first boss after college, and the first person to challenge me on what was really important about Wallace's "project."

Finally, my heartfelt thanks to my mother, Judy Wise, who taught me the joy of reading when I was a child and has, incredibly, never wavered in her support of my ambition to do it for a living.

Notes

FOREWORD

1. René Girard, *A Theater of Envy* (Oxford: Oxford University Press, 1991), 335.
2. Theodor Adorno, "On Jazz," in *Essays on Music*, ed. Richard Leppert, trans. Susan H. Gillespie (Berkeley: University of California Press, 2002), 470–95, 477–78.

INTRODUCTION: HABITS OF MIND

1. Allan Bloom, trans., *The Republic of Plato*, 2nd ed. (New York: Basic Books, 1991), 379a; 607a.
2. "As it seems, whatever looks to be fair to the many who don't know anything—that he will imitate." Bloom, 602b.
3. Bloom, 607a.
4. Jukka Mikkonen, *The Cognitive Value of Philosophical Fiction* (London: Bloomsbury, 2013), 9–10.
5. Stanley Cavell, *The Claim of Reason: Wittgenstein, Skepticism, Morality, and Tragedy* (New York: Oxford University Press, 1979), 496.
6. In the introduction to Wallace's undergraduate thesis on the concept of free will in the philosophy of Richard Taylor—published in 2010 as *Fate, Time and Language*—James Ryerson offers an excellent overview of Wallace's biographical experience with, and comments about, philosophy. Briefly, Wallace seemed headed for a career in analytic philosophy before a "midlife crisis" (14) about the meaningfulness of logic encouraged him to swerve to fiction during his junior year at Amherst. So, alongside his thesis on Taylor, Wallace completed a fiction thesis that would later become his first novel *The Broom of the System* (1987), whose protagonist was the granddaughter of a famous Wittgenstein scholar. After completing an MFA at the University of Arizona and publishing his first two works of fiction, Wallace enrolled at Harvard to

do graduate work in philosophy; he studied there with Stanley Cavell, among others, but left the program when he decided that he "didn't want to be an academic philosopher anymore" (17). In his nonfiction Wallace has covered philosophical topics such as Wittgenstein's private language argument and the afterlife of Roland Barthes's "Death of the Author"; his essays and fiction are studded with references to Kant, Hegel, Wittgenstein, Emerson, and Cavell, among others (Schopenhauer's "The Vanity of Life" was discovered on his desk with the fragments collected in his posthumous novel). He was the author of a book about infinity, *Everything and More: A Compact History of Infinity* (New York: Norton, 2010) and a short story named for Richard Rorty's "Philosophy and the Mirror of Nature." In his book *Understanding David Foster Wallace* (Columbia, SC: University of South Carolina Press, 2003), Marshall Boswell argues that Wittgenstein's theory of language is "the key" to unraveling the mysteries of *The Broom*. More recently, Stephen Mulhall has offered an interpretation of that novel in a similar vein. See Stephen Mulhall, "Quartet: Wallace's Wittgenstein, Moran's Amis," in *The Self and Its Shadows: A Book of Essays on Individuality as Negation in Philosophy and the Arts* (Oxford: Oxford University Press, 2013), 283–320. Wallace's father was a philosophy professor at the University of Illinois and remembers reading Plato's *Phaedo* with his son when David was fourteen years old.

7. Paul Horwich, *Wittgenstein's Metaphilosophy* (Oxford: Oxford University Press, 2013), esp. 6–7.

8. I'm thankful to my colleague Ben Jeffery for sharing a paper on Wittgenstein and Freud that helped me think through this relationship.

9. Ludwig Wittgenstein, *Philosophical Investigations* [1953], trans. G. E. M. Anscombe, 3rd ed. (Upper Saddle River, NJ: Prentice Hall, 1973), §133. The importance of Wittgenstein's notion of a philosophy as a form of therapy has been a source of controversy in Wittgenstein scholarship. The passage quoted here is still ignored by many contemporary philosophers interested in Wittgenstein, but it has received increasing attention in recent decades thanks largely to philosophers like Stanley Cavell and Cora Diamond. In her introduction to a collection of essays entitled *The New Wittgenstein* (New York: Routledge, 2000) Alice Crary describes the selections as agreeing in "suggesting that Wittgenstein's primary aim in philosophy is—to use a word he himself employs in characterizing his later philosophical procedures—a *therapeutic* one" (1). In the *New York Times* blog series *The Stone*, Paul Horwich presents the keystone of Wittgenstein's "notorious doctrine" as being that "a decent approach to [philosophy] must avoid theory-construction and instead be merely 'therapeutic,' confined to exposing the irrational assumptions on which theory-oriented investigations are based and the irrational conclusions to which they lead." Paul Horwich, "Was Wittgenstein Right?" *New York Times*, March 3, 2013, https://opinionator.blogs.nytimes.com/2013/03/03/was-wittgenstein-right. Throughout

this study I will refer to Diamond's, Horwich's, and especially Cavell's glosses on Wittgenstein's later philosophy when they help illuminate how that philosophy resembled what Wallace attempted to do in his fiction.

10. Mark McGurl, "The Institution of Nothing: David Foster Wallace in the Program," *boundary 2* 41, no. 3 (2014): 29.

11. "Uncategorized: Infinite Index." Infinite Summer, June 7, 2010, http://infinitesummer.org.

12. See, e.g., Glenn Kenny, "Why the End of the Tour Isn't Really About My Friend David Foster Wallace," *The Guardian*, July 29, 2015, www.theguardian.com/books/2015/jul/29/why-the-end-of-the-tour-isnt-really-about-my-friend-david-foster-wallace; and Bret Easton Ellis, "Novelist and Screenwriter Bret Easton Ellis (*The Canyons*) Talks James Ponsoldt's *The End of the Tour*," *Talkhouse*, August 11, 2015, http://thetalkhouse.com/film/talks/novelist-and-screenwriter-bret-easton-ellis-the-canyons-talks-james-ponsoldts-the-end-of-the-tour.

13. McGurl, "The Institution of Nothing," 43.

14. In a line of dialogue that's repeated in the movie, Wallace describes his likely readership as "mostly white, upper middle class or upper class, [and] obscenely well educated." David Lipsky, *Although of Course You End Up Becoming Yourself: A Road Trip with David Foster Wallace* (New York: Broadway, 2010), 82.

15. Ed Finn, "Becoming Yourself: The Afterlife of Reception," in *The Legacy of David Foster Wallace*, ed. Samuel Cohen and Lee Konstantinou (Iowa City: University of Iowa Press, 2012), 151–77.

16. Amy Hungerford, "On Not Reading DFW," in *Making Literature Now* (Stanford: Stanford University Press, 2016), 141–68; and Deirdre Coyle, "Men Recommend David Foster Wallace to Me," *Electric Literature*, April 17, 2017, https://electricliterature.com/men-recommend-david-foster-wallace-to-me-7889a9dc6f03.

17. René Descartes, "Meditation Two: Concerning the Nature of the Human Mind: That It Is Better Known Than the Body." In *Meditations, Objections, and Replies*, ed. Roger Ariew and Donald Cress (London: Hackett, 2006), 13.

18. Descartes, 13, 15.

19. Philosophers and intellectual historians have many compelling answers for *why* the Cartesian picture of thinking has become so pervasive in contemporary Western culture: secularization, capitalism, the obvious practical advantages of scientific reason, etc. Taking a cue from the AA portion of *Infinite Jest*, where the addicts are instructed to avoid the wormhole of "why," I will not in this book attempt to provide a causal explanation for how we got here. Rather, I will focus, as Wallace's fiction does, on showing how this picture functions across the various spheres of our society.

20. This goes back to the kind of romantic art that privileges the emotions or the passions over the intellect, but the point can be extended to include much postmodern literary criticism. In recent years a series of challenges to the Cartesian notion of the human as the thinking animal have been united under the title of "affect theory," which has privileged emotional, neurological, or otherwise nonintentional processes over intentional or self-conscious uses of reason.

21. Descartes, "Meditation Two," 17.

22. W. V. Quine, "Semantic Ascent," in *The Linguistic Turn*, ed. Richard Rorty, 2nd ed. (Chicago: University of Chicago Press, 1991), 169.

23. Ludwig Wittgenstein, *Tractatus Logico-Philosophicus* [1921], trans. C. K. Ogden (Denver, CO: Dover, 1998), 6.43.

24. David Foster Wallace, "E Unibus Pluram," in *A Supposedly Fun Thing I'll Never Do Again: Essays and Arguments* (New York: Back Bay, 1998), 67.

25. I am not claiming that Wallace's "treatments" are always, or ever, *successful*. It is impossible to judge to what extent a therapeutic intervention has worked, even in one's own case. But the same may be said for literary criticism that makes other kinds of claims for novels, such as that they constitute a political or a cultural intervention.

26. Robert Pippin, *Modernism as a Philosophical Problem* (Hoboken: Wiley-Blackwell, 1999), 6.

27. See Claire Hayes-Brady, "The Book, the Broom and the Ladder: Philosophical Groundings in the Work of David Foster Wallace," in *Consider David Foster Wallace*, ed. David Hering (Los Angeles: Sideshow Media Group Press, 2010), 24–37, 29; Mary K. Holland, "The Art's Heart's Purpose: Braving the Narcissistic Loop of David Foster Wallace's *Infinite Jest*," *Critique* 41, no. 3 (2006): 218–42; N. Katherine Hayles, "The Illusion of Autonomy and the Fact of Recursivity: Virtual Ecologies, Entertainment, and *Infinite Jest*," *New Literary History* 30, no. 3 (1999): 675–97; and Connie Luther, "David Foster Wallace: Westward with Fredric Jameson," in *Consider David Foster Wallace*, ed. David Hering (Los Angeles: Sideshow Media Group Press, 2010), 49–61, 52.

28. Lee Konstantinou, "No Bull," in *The Legacy of David Foster Wallace*, ed. Samuel Cohen and Lee Konstantinou (Iowa City: University of Iowa Press, 2012), 83–112, 85; Adam Kelly, "David Foster Wallace and the New Sincerity in American Fiction," in *Consider David Foster Wallace*, ed. David Hering (Los Angeles: Sideshow Media Group Press, 2010), 131–47, 145; Timothy Aubry, *Reading as Therapy: What Contemporary Fiction Does for Middle-Class Americans* (Iowa City: University of Iowa Press, 2011); Zadie Smith, *Changing My Mind: Occasional Essays* (New York: Penguin, 2010); Mark McGurl "The Institution of Nothing: David Foster Wallace in the Program," *boundary 2* 41, no. 3 (2014): 27–54.

29. Stephen J. Burn, "Consider David Foster Wallace (Review)," *Modernism/Modernity* 18, no. 2 (2011): 466.

30. Adam Kelly, "David Foster Wallace and the New Sincerity in American Fiction," in *Consider David Foster Wallace*, ed. David Hering (Los Angeles: Sideshow Media Group Press, 2010), 131–47. Kelly expanded on the topic in "Dialectic of Sincerity: Lionel Trilling and David Foster Wallace," *Post45*, Oct. 17, 2014, http://post45.research.yale.edu/2014/10/dialectic-of-sincerity-lionel-trilling-and-david-foster-wallace/. For my purposes, though, the new essay does not add anything of significance to Kelly's original claims about Wallace's conception of sincerity.

31. David Foster Wallace, *Infinite Jest*, 10th anniv. ed. (New York: Back Bay, 2006), 369. Quoted in Kelly, "New Sincerity," 141.

32. Kelly, "New Sincerity," 140, 141.

33. Kelly, 143.

34. Kelly, 140.

35. Kelly, 143, 146.

36. Stanley Cavell, "The Availability of Wittgenstein's Later Philosophy," in *Must We Mean What We Say?* 2nd ed. (Cambridge: Cambridge University Press, 2002), 65.

37. I will discuss the various ways Wallace attempts to communicate this point in Chapter 3. I do think it's important, however, to challenge Kelly's use of one piece of evidence from Wallace's nonfiction, which he uses to support his reading of Wallace's position on authorial intentionality. Kelly notes a distinction Wallace draws, in his review of Bryan A. Garner's *Dictionary of Modern Usage*, between two kinds of appeals a writer can make to his or her readers: the Logical Appeal and the Ethical Appeal. In that essay Wallace praises Garner for making the Ethical Appeal, which he describes as "a complex and sophisticated 'Trust Me.' It's the boldest, most ambitious, and also most democratic of rhetorical appeals because it requires the rhetor to convince us not just of his intellectual acuity or technical competence but of his basic decency and fairness and sensitivity to the audience's own hopes and fears." David Foster Wallace, "Consider the Lobster," in *"Consider the Lobster" and Other Essays* (New York: Back Bay, 2007), 77. Kelly takes this to support his claim that Wallace considers authorial sincerity to be a matter of "Blind Faith" on the part of the reader, but two things about the passage point in a different direction. First, trust and "Blind Faith" are not the same—and the distinction between them makes a difference. Trust is often if not always granted for a reason that can be communicated to another person, even if that person does not agree with the reason, whereas blind faith, by definition, excludes reasons (it is not blind in the relevant sense if there is a reason for it). Wallace's "Trust Me" is therefore not equivalent to Kelly's idea that he is asking the reader to have unquestioning faith in him. Second, Wallace does

not put the burden for determining the validity of the ethical appeal on the *reader*. This does not mean Wallace considers the reader to be an entirely passive member of the author-reader dyad, but in this quotation, particularly, he stresses that it is the ethical author's job to rhetorically *convince* the reader of his decency, fairness, and sensitivity. This means it is his job to give the reader reason to trust him. Trust, that is, is the end result of the Ethical Appeal, not its precondition.

38. Of course, this might be precisely the point. Timothy Aubry, among others, has suggested that part of the motivation behind the questions the New Critics asked about art was to create problems regarding the interpretation of artistic works—problems that required their particular expertise to address. At a time when science was accorded increasing prestige within the university, Aubry argues, this was part of the attempt by literary critics to "establish literary criticism as a legitimate academic field." Timothy Aubry, *Guilty Aesthetic Pleasures* (Cambridge, MA: Harvard University Press, 2018), 53.

39. Wittgenstein, *Philosophical Investigations*, §308.

40. "It may easily look as if every doubt merely revealed an existing gap in the foundations; so that secure understanding is only possible if we first doubt everything that can be doubted, and then remove all these doubts" (Wittgenstein, *Philosophical Investigations*, §87).

41. Sigmund Freud and Joseph Breuer, *Studies in Hysteria* [1895], trans. Nicola Luckhurst (New York: Penguin, 2004), 306 [Translation slightly altered: *common* and *ordinary* are both frequent translations of the Austrian.].

42. Coyle, "Men Recommend David Foster Wallace."

43. Hungerford, *Making Literature Now*, 141, 147.

44. Jonathan Franzen, "Farther Away," in *Farther Away* (New York: Farrar, Straus and Giroux, 2012}, 41.

45. McGurl, "The Institution of Nothing," 33.

46. Plato, *Republic*, 600e.

CHAPTER 1. NARRATIVE MORALITY

1. Elizabeth S. Anker and Rita Felski, eds., *Critique and Postcritique* (Durham, NC: Duke University Press, 2017), 3.

2. See Stephen Best and Sharon Marcus, "Surface Reading: An Introduction," *Representations* 108, no. 1 (2009): 16.

3. Merve Emre, *Paraliterary* (Chicago: University of Chicago Press, 2017), 255.

4. Timothy Aubry, *Guilty Aesthetic Pleasures* (Cambridge, MA: Harvard University Press, 2018), 13.

5. Toril Moi, *Revolution of the Ordinary: Literary Studies After Wittgenstein, Cavell, and Austin* (Chicago: University of Chicago Press, 2017).

6. Toril Moi, "Nothing Is Hidden," in *Critique and Postcritique*, ed. Elizabeth S. Anker and Rita Felski (Durham, NC: Duke University Press, 2017), 39.

7. Toril Moi, "Describing My Struggle," *The Point*, Dec. 2017, https://thepointmag.com/2017/criticism/describing-my-struggle-knausgaard.

8. G. E. M. Anscombe, "Modern Moral Philosophy" [1958], in *Human Life, Action, and Ethics: Essays by G. E. M. Anscombe*, ed. Mary Geach and Luke Gormally (Exeter: Imprint Academic, 2006), 169–95.

9. Iris Murdoch, *The Sovereignty of Good* [1970] (New York: Routledge, 2001), 17–23.

10. Murdoch, 26. Cora Diamond makes a similar point when she describes the proper task of what she calls "realistic" philosophy as being to allow us to see (and see through) the "illusion" that philosophy is "an area of inquiry, in the sense in which we are familiar with it"—meaning the scientific sense. See Cora Diamond, "Realism and the Realistic Spirit," in *The Realistic Spirit: Wittgenstein, Philosophy, and the Mind* (Cambridge, MA: MIT Press, 1995), 69–70.

11. "We must do away with all *explanation*, and description alone must take its place." Ludwig Wittgenstein, *Philosophical Investigations* [1953], trans. G. E. M. Anscombe, 3rd ed. (Upper Saddle River, NJ: Prentice Hall, 1973), §109.

12. Wittgenstein, §129.

13. Wittgenstein, §125, §127.

14. The formulation may bring to mind another philosopher whose approach to literature was influenced by Wittgenstein's emphasis on redescription, Richard Rorty.

15. Robert Pippin, *Henry James and Modern Moral Life* (Cambridge: Cambridge University Press, 2000), 98.

16. Pippin, 56.

17. Pippin, 5, 10.

18. One could easily perform a similar analysis of contemporary Wallace criticism, much of which draws lessons about his characters based on what we know of Wallace's own troubled and highly eccentric life.

19. Robert Pippin, "On 'Becoming Who One Is' (and Failing): Proust's Problematic Selves," in *The Persistence of Subjectivity* (Cambridge: Cambridge University Press, 2003), 321.

20. Pippin, *Henry James*, 96.

21. See G. W. F. Hegel, *Aesthetics: Lectures on Fine Art* [1835], trans. T. M. Knox (Oxford: Oxford University Press, 1998), 1:10–14.

22. Pippin, *Henry James*, 173.

23. Pippin, 175.

24. Pippin, 55 (italics in original).

25. Stanley Cavell, "The Avoidance of Love: A Reading of *King Lear*," in

Must We Mean What We Say? 2nd ed. (Cambridge: Cambridge University Press, 2002), 313.

26.   Stanley Cavell, "Ending the Waiting Game, " in *Must We Mean What We Say?* 2nd ed. (Cambridge: Cambridge University Press, 2002), 119.

27.   Cavell "The Avoidance of Love," 310.

28.   When calling Cavell's approach to literature "psychoanalytic," it is important to distinguish it from how that school of criticism is conventionally construed. Psychoanalytic literary criticism has consisted mostly in turning authors or their characters into clinical case studies and looking to psychoanalytic theory for answers to the mysteries of their behavior or motivations. Cavell's discussions of literature *are* influenced by Freud but not in this direction, and his readings share little with those of the canonical psychoanalytic critics like Ernest Jones and Janet Adelman. In Cavell's best readings the goal is not to psychoanalyze the characters or the author so much as it is to psychoanalyze the interaction (strange as it sounds) between the work and its audience.

29.   Cavell, "The Avoidance of Love," 290.

30.   Cavell, "Ending the Waiting Game," 119.

31.   Cavell, 117.

32.   Cavell, 131.

33.   Some of these formulations can make Cavell sound perilously close to a deconstructionist. In fact, therapeutic criticism could not be farther, in ambition and method, from deconstruction. Whereas the deconstructionists tended to suspect the work of art—or the artist—of being ideological, therapeutic criticism suspects the *reader* of being ideological or, at least, stuck in habits of thinking and reading that prevent her or him from seeing what the artist is trying to say. Cavell's distance from the dominant trends in critical theory has been theorized by some to account for his relative neglect in literature departments. See, e.g., Richard Eldridge and Bernard Rhie, "Cavell, Literary Studies, and the Human Subject," in *Stanley Cavell and Literary Studies* (London: Bloomsbury, 2011), 1–13.

34.   Moi, "Nothing Is Hidden," 37.

35.   Stanley Cavell, "A Matter of Meaning It," in *Must We Mean What We Say?* 2nd ed. (Cambridge: Cambridge University Press, 2002), 37.

36.   Murdoch, *The Sovereignty of Good*, 65; Wittgenstein, *Philosophical Investigations*, §133. See also Cavell: "Our investigation gets its importance from what it destroys, and in particular from its destruction of a construction of fantasy, precisely a fantasy of importance." Stanley Cavell, *A Pitch of Philosophy: Autobiographical Exercises* (Cambridge, MA: Harvard University Press, 1994), 75.

37.   Toril Moi, "The Adventure of Reading," in *Stanley Cavell and Literary Studies* (London: Bloomsbury, 2011), 18.

38. Stanley Cavell, "Aesthetic Problems of Modern Philosophy," in *Must We Mean What We Say?* 2nd ed. (Cambridge: Cambridge University Press, 2002), 84; and Stanley Cavell, *In Quest of the Ordinary* (Chicago: University of Chicago Press, 1994), 12.

39. Wittgenstein, *Philosophical Investigations*, §287.

40. Meredith Rand in *The Pale King* (New York: Back Bay Books, 2012), 496.

CHAPTER 2. PLAYING GAMES

1. Stephen J. Burn, *David Foster Wallace's "Infinite Jest": A Reader's Guide* (London: Bloomsbury, 2003), 10.

2. Michiko Kakutani, "A Country Dying of Laughter," review of *Infinite Jest*, *New York Times*, Feb. 13, 1996, www.nytimes.com/1996/02/13/books/books-of-the-times-a-country-dying-of-laughter-in-1079-pages.html.

3. James Wood, "Human, All Too Inhuman," *New Republic*, July 24, 2000, https://newrepublic.com/article/61361/human-inhuman.

4. The books are Burn's *Reader's Guide* and Boswell's *Understanding David Foster Wallace* (Columbia: University of South Carolina Press, 2003).

5. Lee Konstantinou, "Wipe That Smirk off Your Face: Postironic Literature and the Politics of Character" (PhD diss., Stanford University, 2009).

6. Adam Kelly, "David Foster Wallace and the New Sincerity in American Fiction," in *Consider David Foster Wallace*, ed. David Hering (Los Angeles: Sideshow Media Group Press, 2010), 131–47.

7. Timothy Aubry, *Reading as Therapy* (Iowa City: University of Iowa Press, 2011).

8. N. Katherine Hayles, "The Illusion of Autonomy and the Fact of Recursivity: Virtual Ecologies, Entertainment, and *Infinite Jest*," *New Literary History* 30, no. 3 (1999): 675–97.

9. Konstantinou, Wipe That Smirk," 156, 155.

10. David Foster Wallace, "Joseph Frank's Dostoevsky," in *Consider the Lobster and Other Essays* (New York: Back Bay, 2007), 271.

11. Henceforth "Wallace's AA," to be clear that I am referring to the presentation of AA within the novel, not to the organization itself. I have no reason to doubt the accuracy of Wallace's depiction of AA, but I am not in a position to evaluate where it might be inaccurate, nor would such discrepancies be of concern to me here.

12. Although it is that. For example, "Each language partner, when a 'move' pertaining to him is made, undergoes a 'displacement,' an alteration of some kind that not only affects him in his capacity as addressee and referent, but also as sender. These 'moves' necessarily provoke 'countermoves.'" This is how Lyotard describes a conversation in *The Postmodern Condition: A Report on Knowledge* (Minneapolis: University of Minnesota Press, 1984), 16.

13. See especially the novella "Westward the Course of Empire Takes Its Way," in Wallace's first short story collection, *Girl with Curious Hair* (New York: Norton, 1989), 231–373; and his well-received essay "E Unibus Pluram: Television and U.S. Fiction," originally published in the *Review of Contemporary Fiction* 13, no. 2 (1993): 151–94, before being collected in David Foster Wallace, *A Supposedly Fun Thing I'll Never Do Again* (New York: Back Bay, 1998), 21–82 (citations are from the latter). I discuss Wallace and irony specifically in "Death Is Not the End," *The Point*, no. 1 (2009) https://thepointmag.com/2009/criticism/death-is-not-the-end.

14. AA has been attacked for being "unscientific" throughout its history, most recently by Gabrielle Glaser in *The Atlantic*, who intoned that "the problem is that nothing about the 12-step approach draws on modern science." Gabrielle Glaser, "The Irrationality of Alcoholics Anonymous," *The Atlantic*, April 2015, www.theatlantic.com/magazine/archive/2015/04/the-irrationality -of-alcoholics-anonymous/386255. For Wallace, this is precisely what makes it so promising as a counterweight to contemporary forms of despair.

15. Robert Pippin, *Modernism as a Philosophical Problem: On the Dissatisfactions of European High Culture*, 2nd ed. (London: Wiley-Blackwell, 1999), 6, 4.

16. René Descartes, *Discourse on Method* [1637] (London: Penguin, 2003), 87; Virginia Woolf, "Modern Fiction" [1925], in *The Common Reader* (Wilmington, MA: Mariner, 2002), 152; James Joyce, "Letter to Lady Gregory" [1902], in *Selected Letters of James Joyce*, ed. Richard Ellman (London: Faber and Faber, 2003), 8.

17. Jean Baudrillard, *The Ecstasy of Communication* (Cambridge, MA: MIT Press, 2012), 26; Fredric Jameson, "Postmodernism and Consumer Society," Whitney Museum transcript, 1982, 4; Michel Foucault, *Discipline and Punish*, trans. Alan Sheridan (New York: Vintage, 1995), 30.

18. A description of people that, as Burn points out, is "revealingly empty of human agency" (Burn, *David Foster Wallace's "Infinite Jest,"* 39).

19. Burn, 44.

20. Samuel Cohen, "To Wish to Try to Sing to the Next Generation: *Infinite Jest*'s History," in *The Legacy of David Foster Wallace*, ed. Samuel Cohen and Lee Konstantinou (Iowa City: University of Iowa Press, 2012), 67.

21. Besides Shakespeare's Prince Hal, and Hamlet, Hal's name and situation call to mind Stanley Kubrick's *2001: A Space Odyssey* and its "HAL 9000." Hence the significance of the eyes as "zeros"—as well as one inflection on Hal's (upcoming) denial that he is "not a machine." HAL 9000 articulates essentially the same denial when it is being dismantled in *2001*. (Of course HAL 9000 *is* a machine.)

22. Cohen, "To Wish," 67–77.

23. Stanley Cavell, *Must We Mean What We Say?* 2nd ed. (Cambridge: Cambridge University Press, 2002), 212.

24. Compare to Hamlet's saying to his mother that he has in him "that which surpasseth show," while in both cases what lies outside the subject is presented as threateningly corrupt, toxic, or "rotten."

25. Burn points to a passage later in the book—but much earlier chronologically—in which Hal's father, James Incandenza, is informed by *his* father that, if he wants to make it as an athlete, he'll have to accept the "hard news" that he's "a body." If this might be taken as a garden-variety cliché, he clarifies that he means it all the way down, telling his ten-year-old son, "That quick little scientific-prodigy's mind [your mother]'s so proud of and won't quit twittering about: son it's just neural spasms, those thoughts in your mind are just the sound of your head revving, and head is still just body, Jim. Commit this to memory. Head is body. Jim, brace yourself against my shoulders here for this hard news, at ten: you're a machine" (*IJ*, 159, quoted in Burn, *David Foster Wallace's "Infinite Jest,"* 43).

26. "Schtitt was educated in pre-Unification *Gymnasium* under the rather Kanto-Hegelian idea that jr. athletics was about learning to sacrifice the hot narrow imperatives of the self—the needs, the desires, the fears, the multiform cravings of the individual appetitive will—to the larger imperatives of a team (OK, the state) and a set of delimiting rules (OK, the Law)" (*IJ* 83).

27. See Aaron Swartz, "What Happens at the End of *Infinite Jest?*" *Raw Thoughts* (blog), Sept. 16, 2009, www.aaronsw.com/weblog/ijend.

28. "Wittgenstein's motive," Cavell writes, "is to put the human animal back into language and therewith back into philosophy." Stanley Cavell, *The Claim of Reason: Wittgenstein, Skepticism, Morality, and Tragedy* (New York: Oxford University Press, 1979), 207. This assumes what Cavell says elsewhere—that modern philosophy has somehow exiled the "human." And one of the places he thinks it has lived in exile is in literature, especially in the literature known as romanticism. (See also Cavell, 83–84.)

29. Descartes, "Dedicatory Letter," in *Meditations on First Philosophy*, ed. John Cottingham (Cambridge: Cambridge University Press, 2017), 3.

30. "Today, from any number of distinct perspectives, the social theorists, the psychoanalysts, even the linguists . . . are all exploring the notion that that kind of individualism and personal identity is a thing of the past; that the old individual or individualist subject is 'dead'; and that one might even describe the concept of the unique individual and the theoretical basis of individualism as ideological." Jameson, "Postmodernism and Consumer Society," 1–2.

31. If Hobbes is the theorist of a society that does not acknowledge the inner or authentic individual at all, then Rousseau would seem to pit the inner, unknowable individual against a cold and inhuman society. Whereas Hobbes denies the gap between individual and society, Rousseau makes it unbridgeable.

32. Two other well-known postmodern novels—DeLillo's *Great Jones*

Street and Pynchon's *Gravity's Rainbow*—end rather than begin with characters suddenly unable to express themselves. Interestingly, in both of those cases—and in contrast to Hal's—the character in question feels his dumbness to be a *relief*, as if he has finally gotten what he was after.

33. Hayles, "The Illusion of Autonomy," 695.

34. Frank Cioffi, "'An Anguish Become Thing': Narrative as Performance in David Foster Wallace's *Infinite Jest.*" *Narrative* 8, no. 2 (2000): 161–81.

35. Mary K. Holland, "The Art's Heart's Purpose: Braving the Narcissistic Loop of David Foster Wallace's *Infinite Jest,*" *Critique* 41, no. 3 (2006): 218–42.

36. Cavell, *Must We Mean What We Say?* 85.

37. Holland, "The Art's Heart's Purpose," 233.

38. Ludwig Wittgenstein, *Philosophical Investigations* [1953], trans. G. E. M. Anscombe, 3rd ed. (Upper Saddle River, NJ: Prentice Hall, 1973), §133.

39. Konstantinou, "Wipe That Smirk," 125.

40. Hayles, "The Illusion of Autonomy," 693 (my italics).

41. Aubry, *Reading as Therapy*, 99, 109, 113. The Scott article is "The Panic of Influence," *New York Review of Books*, Feb. 10, 2000. Wallace *does* want us to see that our relationship to certain aesthetic habits bears comparison to the relationship that addicts have with their substances. Whether he himself is addicted to those habits is another matter.

42. It is not just *drug addicts* who are known for "making finer and finer distinctions about a situation" while "failing catastrophically" to intervene in it.

43. Elaine Blair, "A New Brilliant Start," *New York Review of Books*, Dec. 6, 2012, www.nybooks.com/articles/2012/12/06/new-brilliant-start.

44. Blair.

45. Wittgenstein, *Philosophical Investigations*, §127.

46. "When we do philosophy we are like savages, primitive people, who hear the expressions of civilized men, put a false interpretation on them, and then draw the queerest conclusions from it." Wittgenstein, *Philosophical Investigations*, §194. Some of my own thinking on this topic has been influenced by Rush Rhees's essay "Language: A Family of Games?" in *Wittgenstein and the Possibility of Discourse*, ed. D. Z. Phillips (Oxford: Wiley-Blackwell, 1998), 116–30.

47. Again, Wallace was not thinking only of drug addicts or clinical cases when he had a doctor observe, early on in the novel, that "sarcasm and jokes were often the bottle in which clinical depressives sent out their most plangent screams for someone to care and help them" (*IJ* 71).

48. Wallace, "E Unibus Pluram," 81.

49. One of the things you learn at Ennet House is that "logical validity is no guarantee of truth" (*IJ*, 202).

50. Aubry, *Reading as Therapy*, 99. Specifically, Aubry interprets Wallace as endorsing conventional therapy's "presumption of the psychological as a space of depth and fascination that can rival the aesthetic or the philosophical."

51. Stanley Cavell, "Aesthetic Problems of Modern Philosophy," in *Must We Mean What We Say?* 2nd ed. (Cambridge: Cambridge University Press, 2002), 85–86.

52. Wittgenstein, *Philosophical Investigations*, §116.

53. Wittgenstein, §118.

54. Sigmund Freud and Joseph Breuer, *Studies in Hysteria* [1895], trans. Nicola Luckhurst (New York: Penguin, 2004), 306.

CHAPTER 3. SO DECIDE

1. Deirdre Coyle, "Men Recommend David Foster Wallace to Me," *Electric Literature*, April 17, 2017, https://electricliterature.com/men-recommend-david-foster-wallace-to-me-7889a9dc6f03.

2. "No doubt these portraits are meant as sardonic commentaries on our narcissistic, therapeutic age, but they are so long-winded, so solipsistic, so predictable in their use of irony and gratuitous narrative high jinks that they end up being as tiresome and irritating as their subjects." Michiko Kakutani, "Calling Them Misogynists Would Be Too Kind," review of *Brief Interviews with Hideous Men*, New York Times, June 1, 1999, www.nytimes.com/1999/06/01/books/books-of-the-times-calling-them-misogynists-would-be-too-kind.html.

3. A. O. Scott, "The Panic of Influence," *New York Review of Books*, Feb. 10, 2000, www.nybooks.com/articles/2000/02/10/the-panic-of-influence.

4. Amy Hungerford, "On Not Reading DFW," in *Making Literature Now* (Stanford: Stanford University Press, 2016), 160.

5. The same pattern emerges in a different context—one where gender plays a less conspicuous role—in one of *Brief Interviews*' most famous stories, "The Depressed Person" (*BI* 31–58). There, the protagonist is a woman in "terrible and unceasing emotional pain." The story appears at first to be about her attempts, in conversations with her therapist and the "support system" of friends the therapist encourages her to cultivate, to find the right explanation for her pain. In one fusillade of postmodern therapeutic jargon after another, the woman diagnoses herself and her various defense mechanisms, bemoaning in each case the ability of the explanation to make her feel any better. In subtle and not-so-subtle ways, however, the story suggests that the depressed person's pain is related less to her inability to explain it accurately than to her inability to stop trying to explain it. It is the depressed person's obsession with discovering such an explanation that keeps her from noticing when those around her—e.g., her therapist and the "core members" of her support system—experience their own pain and suffering. Such failures of empathy, resulting from an inability to see those around her as anything other than stepping stones for her own self-growth, are what connect the depressed person to the hideous men.

6. Published as "Certainly the End of *Something* or Other, One Would Sort of Have to Think," in *"Consider the Lobster" and Other Essays* (New York: Back Bay, 2007), 51–60.

7. These writers do not treat women in the same way in every respect, of course. Still, their most famous books are always about men, and usually they are about men attempting to free themselves from the constraints imposed on them by women (and sometimes children). Updike's Rabbit tetralogy may be the signal example, but Roth's *Portnoy's Complaint* and *Sabbath's Theater*, as virtual bookends to his career, are not far behind. Bellow's *Humboldt's Gift* follows the same pattern, while Mailer's *American Dream* may be the most baroque and disturbing example of them all. All four novelists provide templates from which Wallace could have drawn in imagining his hideous men.

8. Patricia Waugh, *Metafiction: The Theory and Practice of Self-Conscious Fiction* (New York: Routledge, 1984), 2.

9. David Foster Wallace, "E Unibus Pluram: Television and U.S. Fiction," in *A Supposedly Fun Thing I'll Never Do Again* (New York: Back Bay, 1998), 21–82.

10. Water plays an important symbolic function throughout Wallace's fiction and nonfiction, culminating in his famous Kenyon commencement speech, entitled "This Is Water." See David Foster Wallace, *This Is Water: Some Thoughts, Delivered on a Significant Occasion, About Living a Compassionate Life* (New York: Little, Brown, 2009). In a later story in *Brief Interviews*, "Church Not Made with Hands," a little girl gets sucked into the drain of a backyard pool while her mother, who can't swim, watches helplessly from the side (*BI* 165–80).

11. Iannis Goerlandt, "'This Is Not Wholly True': Notes on Annotation in David Foster Wallace's Shorter Fiction (and Non-Fiction)," in *Consider David Foster Wallace*, ed. David Hering (Los Angeles: Sideshow Media Group Press, 2010), 165.

12. The public pool is the location of history (Marco Polo, cannonballs) and nature (sharks, minnows), as well as the trivial everyday (dives, corner tags).

13. Zadie Smith, *Changing My Mind: Occasional Essays* (New York: Penguin, 2009), 266.

14. Smith, 264.

15. The two most serious works of criticism on *Brief Interviews*—Smith's *Changing My Mind*; and Stephen Mulhall's "Quartet: Wallace's Wittgenstein, Moran's Amis," in *The Self and Its Shadows: A Book of Essays on Individuality as Negation in Philosophy and the Arts* (Oxford: Oxford University Press, 2013)—both treat "Octet" as central, finding in it Wallace's theory of fiction and the final test of whether the reader will have "faith in the agenda of the consciousness behind the text" (Smith, 287). Mulhall be-

gins his close reading of the story by observing that it appears "at the centre" (310) of the collection.

16. "Problems" takes the form of a series of word problems, some involving practical conundrums (how can A time his visit to his Laundromat and his therapist?), some having to do with conflicting desires ("During the night, A, though sleeping with B, dreams of C"), before concluding by asking the reader what "feels wrong" about a scenario in which most of A's practical problems, at least, have been resolved. Updike's story thus hints at what one suspects the author may think of as the truth about our modern social condition: that even after the end of history, society remains incapable of satisfying our real needs. Wallace's "quizzes" are also about our needs, but they confront those needs on a whole different—I want to say on a philosophically therapeutic—level. One of the things *his* quizzes are meant to test is what constitutes our real needs, as opposed to those whims and preferences that merely *present* themselves as needs: "One might say: the axis of reference of our examination must be rotated, but about the fixed point of our real need." Ludwig Wittgenstein, *Philosophical Investigations* [1953], trans. G. E. M. Anscombe, 3rd ed. (Upper Saddle River, NJ: Prentice Hall, 1973), §108.

17. We can only infer, based on what we have here—although it is impossible not to think of some of Wallace's other treatments of addiction—the serial selfishness and solipsism that has led the terminal drug addicts to their current pass, and which make such an act of selflessness even more extraordinary and "self"-sacrificial.

18. Mulhall, "Quartet," 318.

19. Mulhall "Quartet," 317.

20. Wittgenstein, *Philosophical Investigations*, §127.

21. Mulhall, "Quartet," 319.

22. Adam Kelly, "David Foster Wallace and the New Sincerity in American Fiction," in *Consider David Foster Wallace*, ed. David Hering (Los Angeles: Sideshow Media Group Press, 2010), 145.

23. Smith, *Changing My Mind*, 287.

24. The way Kelly and Mulhall misread the end of "Octet" is reminiscent of the way some philosophical commentators often (mis)read two comments of Wittgenstein's. The first is, "Explanations come to an end somewhere"; the second is, "If I have exhausted the justifications, I have reached bedrock and my spade is turned. Then I am inclined to say: 'This is simply what I do.'" Some critics have read these comments as if Wittgenstein is saying that there are certain times we simply have to throw up our arms and leave things, anti-intellectually, up to fate or tradition. As in Wallace's case, the misreading reinscribes the dichotomy that the author is attempting to undermine. To admit that we cannot always explain or justify our actions is not the same as admitting that our actions are senseless or thoughtless or that we bear no responsibility for

them. Nor need we view blind faith as the only alternative to explanation or justification. I do not take this family of remarks as wanting to deny the role explanation plays in our decisions, so much as wanting to bring out how often it is unable to *settle* them—as well as to account for the suffering we cause ourselves and others when we fool ourselves into thinking it can.

25. Christoforos Diakoulakis, "'Quote Unquote Love . . . a Type of Scotopia': David Foster Wallace's *Brief Interviews with Hideous Men*," in *Consider David Foster Wallace*, ed. David Hering (Los Angeles: Sideshow Media Group Press, 2010), 153.

26. Diakoulakis, 153.

27. Smith, *Changing my Mind*, 268 (Smith's italics).

28. Smith, 294.

29. Wittgenstein, *Philosophical Investigations*, §122.

30. Randy Ramal, "Beyond Philosophy: David Foster Wallace on Literature, Wittgenstein, and the Dangers of Theorizing," in *Gesturing Toward Reality: David Foster Wallace and Philosophy* (New York: Bloomsbury, 2014), 189.

31. Stanley Cavell, "Declining Decline: Wittgenstein as a Philosopher of Culture," in *This New Yet Unapproachable America: Lectures After Emerson After Wittgenstein* (Chicago: University of Chicago Press, 2013), 38.

CHAPTER 4. UNTRENDY PROBLEMS

1. Jon Baskin, "Death Is Not the End," *The Point*, Spring 2009, https://thepointmag.com/2009/criticism/death-is-not-the-end

2. Hubert Dreyfus and Sean Dorrance Kelly, *All Things Shining: Reading the Western Classics to Find Meaning in a Secular Age* (New York: Free Press, 2011), 22.

3. Jonathan Franzen, "Farther Away," in *Farther Away: Essays* (New York: Farrar, Straus and Giroux, 2012), 39.

4. Gerald Howard, "I Know Why Bret Easton Ellis Hates David Foster Wallace." *Salon*, Sept. 7, 2012, www.salon.com/2012/09/07/i_know_why _bret_easton_ellis_hates_david_foster_wallace.

5. Dreyfus and Kelly, for instance, intersperse their chapter with paragraph-length descriptions of the depression that led to Wallace's suicide.

6. See, e.g., *Rethinking Therapeutic Culture*, ed. Timothy Aubry and Trysh Travis (Chicago: University of Chicago Press, 2015), 1.

7. Stanley Cavell, *The Claim of Reason: Wittgenstein, Skepticism, Morality, and Tragedy* (New York: Oxford University Press, 1979), 124.

8. Ludwig Wittgenstein, *Philosophical Investigations* [1953], trans. G. E. M. Anscombe, 3rd ed. (Upper Saddle River, NJ: Prentice Hall, 1973), §90.

9. Wittgenstein, 178.

10. I am thinking of Wittgenstein's claim, which comes right above the already-quoted portion of §133 in the *Philosophical Investigations*, that, using

his method of philosophy, "philosophical problems should completely disappear." The line can look very different, depending on whether you emphasize the word *problems* or—as has been customary in English translations—the word *completely*.

11. Wallace described having had the same feeling while writing fiction in college, as reported in D. T. Max, *Every Love Story Is a Ghost Story* (New York: Penguin, 2012), 167.

12. In "E Unibus Pluram" Wallace writes of television actors who carry the "Emersonian holiday" in their eye—that is, "the promise of a vacation from human self-consciousness. Not worrying about how you come across. A total unallergy to gazes. It is contemporarily heroic. It is frightening and strong. It is also, of course, an act" (*SFT* 25). This "self-conscious appearance of unself-consciousnes," Wallace said, was the "the real door" to TV's "hall of mirrors" appeal. The connection of Emerson to acting is itself borrowed from Cavell's *Pursuits of Happiness*, according to Paul Giles, "All Swallowed Up," in *The Legacy of David Foster Wallace*, ed. Samuel Cohen and Lee Konstantinou (Iowa City: University of Iowa Press, 2012), 9.

13. Stanley Cavell, *Conditions Handsome and Unhandsome: The Constitution of Emersonian Perfectionism* (Chicago: University of Chicago Press, 1990), 2, 7.

14. "If any of us knew what we were doing, or where we are going, then when we think we best know!" Ralph Waldo Emerson, "Experience," in *The Essential Writings of Ralph Waldo Emerson*, ed. Brooks Atkinson (New York: Modern Library, 2000), 307–8.

15. Thoreau, "Walden" [1854], in *"Walden" and Other Writings* (New York: Bantam, 2004), 8.

16. Thoreau, 311.

17. Cavell, *Conditions Handsome and Unhandsome*, 58.

18. See Nikil Saval, *Cubed: A Secret History of the Workplace* (2014): "After such knowledge as 'Office Space,' what forgiveness?" (283).

19. Mark McGurl, "The Institution of Nothing: David Foster Wallace in the Program," *boundary 2* 41, no. 3 (2014): 35.

20. McGurl, 35n18.

21. David Foster Wallace, *This Is Water: Some Thoughts, Delivered on a Significant Occasion, About Living a Compassionate Life* (New York: Little, Brown, 2009), 91.

22. In a fragment, an anonymous IRS auditor describes a play he would like to write about life at the IRS. The play, he says, would be a "totally real, true-to-life play. It would be unperformable, that was part of the point." An auditor would sit at a desk in front of a bare wall. "At first there was a clock behind him, but I cut the clock." Then: "He sits there longer and longer until the audience gets more and more bored and restless, and finally they start

leaving, first just a few and then the whole audience, whispering to each other how boring and terrible the play is. Then, once the audience have all left, the real action of the play can start" (*PK* 106).

23. The auditor/playwright never writes his unperformable play because "I could never decide on the action, if there was any, if it's a realistic play" (*PK* 106). The idea might be profitably connected with Kierkegaard's suggestion, in *Either/Or*, that what's *really real* (so to speak) cannot be dramatized; it can only be lived.

24. Cavell, *Conditions Handsome and Unhandsome*, 2.

25. I have stolen this description of Wittgenstein's ambitions from Cavell. My favorite of Cavell's many evocative descriptions of Wittgenstein's project comes in his autobiography, where he calls "the subject sketched in Wittgenstein's *Philosophical Investigations* the subject perpetually seeking peace, therefore endlessly homeless." Stanley Cavell, *Little Did I Know: Excerpts from Memory* (Stanford: Stanford University Press, 2010), 100.

26. Commentators have often described Wallace's trepidation about writing fiction that was too morally or spiritually direct as stemming from his fear of appearing sentimental or moralistic or of disappointing the sophisticated audience he had built up with his early fiction. Wallace sometimes described the struggle that way himself. But it can also be conceived of as a struggle between conflicting intellectual commitments—on the one hand, Wallace's commitment to the idea that literature should be morally edifying for a large audience; on the other hand, his commitment to Wittgenstein's eloquent argument (made especially at the end of the *Tractatus* and in his "Lecture on Ethics") that ethical and spiritual matters should be approached in language only indirectly, if at all.

27. Thoreau, "Walden," 4, 5, 6, 8.

28. Jonathan Raban, "Divine Drudgery," *New York Review of Books*, May 2011, www.nybooks.com/articles/2011/05/12/divine-drudgery.

29. Søren Kierkegaard, *Either/Or: A Fragment of Life* [1843], trans. Alastair Hannay (New York: Penguin, 1992), 460.

30. Lee Konstantinou, *Cool Characters: Irony and American Fiction* (Cambridge, MA: Harvard University Press, 2016), 168.

31. Cavell, *Conditions Handsome and Unhandsome*, 51–52.

32. Cavell, *Conditions Handsome and Unhandsome*, 16.

33. This word surfaces several times in *The Pale King*, usually in the context of a character about to make a major change in her or his life. *Primed* is also "one of the IRS words for putting Examiners in a state where they pay maximum attention to returns" (*PK* 540).

CONCLUSION. IN HEAVEN AND EARTH

1. Stanley Cavell, *Conditions Handsome and Unhandsome: The Constitution of Emersonian Perfectionism* (Chicago: University of Chicago Press, 1990), 7.

2. Cavell, 5.

3. William Shakespeare, *Hamlet*, ed. Ann Thompson and Neil Taylor, 3rd ed. (London: Arden Shakespeare, 2006), 1.5.165–66.

4. Much of what I say in this and the following two paragraphs was shaped by conversations and courses with Irad Kimhi, a philosopher who I can only hope will someday publish his incredibly generative insights about the relationship between philosophy and art. What follows should not be taken as any kind of definitive statement on Professor Kimhi's ideas: I do not want to speak for him, and it is likely that he would disagree with or qualify much of what I say here. But my own thinking is indebted to my time with him at the University of Chicago from 2012 to 2015.

5. *Hamlet*, 1.5.163–66.

6. Stanley Cavell, "The Political and the Psychological," in *Disowning Knowledge in Seven Plays of Shakespeare*, updated ed. (Cambridge: Cambridge University Press, 2003), 162.

7. Stanley Cavell, "Hamlet's Burden of Proof," in *Disowning Knowledge in Seven Plays of Shakespeare*, updated ed. (Cambridge: Cambridge University Press, 2003), 186.

8. Harold Bloom, *Hamlet: Poem Unlimited* (New York: Riverhead, 2004), 131. In a direct response to Cavell and many others Bloom chides commentators for making "too much" of Hamlet's mourning.

9. Bloom, 119.

Bibliography

Anker, Elizabeth S., and Rita Felski, eds. *Critique and Postcritique.* Durham, NC: Duke University Press, 2017.

Anscombe, G. E. M. "Modern Moral Philosophy." 1958. In *Human Life, Action and Ethics: Essays by G. E. M. Anscombe,* edited by Mary Geach and Luke Gormally, 169–95. Exeter: Imprint Academic, 2006.

Armstrong, Nancy. *How Novels Think: The Limits of Individualism from 1719–1900.* New York: Columbia University Press, 2006.

Aubry, Timothy. *Guilty Aesthetic Pleasures.* Cambridge, MA: Harvard University Press, 2018.

———. *Reading as Therapy: What Contemporary Fiction Does for Middle-Class Americans.* Iowa City: University of Iowa Press, 2011.

Aubry, Timothy, and Trysh Travis. *Rethinking Therapeutic Culture.* Chicago: University of Chicago Press, 2015.

Baskin, Jon. "Death Is Not the End." *The Point,* Spring 2009, https://thepoint mag.com/2009/criticism/death-is-not-the-end.

———. "Untrendy Problems: *The Pale King's* Philosophical Inspirations." In Bolger and Korb, *Gesturing Toward Reality,* 141–57.

Baudrillard, Jean. *The Ecstasy of Communication.* Cambridge, MA: MIT Press, 2012.

Best, Stephen, and Sharon Marcus. "Surface Reading: An Introduction." *Representations* 108, no. 1 (2009): 1–21.

Birkerts, Sven. "The Alchemist's Retort: A Multi-layered Postmodern Saga of Damnation and Salvation." *The Atlantic,* Feb. 1996, www.theatlantic.com/magazine/archive/1996/02/the-alchemists-retort/376533.

Blair, Elaine. "A New Brilliant Start." *New York Review of Books,* Dec. 6, 2012. www.nybooks.com/articles/2012/12/06/new-brilliant-start.

Bloom, Allan, trans. *The Republic of Plato.* 2nd ed. New York: Basic Books, 1991.

Bloom, Harold. *Hamlet: Poem Unlimited*. New York: Riverhead, 2003.

———. *William Shakespeare's "Hamlet."* Langhorne, PA: Chelsea House, 1996.

Bolger, Robert K., and Scott Korb, eds. *Gesturing Toward Reality: David Foster Wallace and Philosophy*. New York: Bloomsbury, 2014.

Boswell, Marshall, ed. *David Foster Wallace and "The Long Thing": New Essays on the Novels*. London: Bloomsbury, 2014.

———. "Trickle-Down Citizenship: Taxes and Civic Responsibility in *The Pale King*." In Boswell, *David Foster Wallace*, 209–26.

———. *Understanding David Foster Wallace*. Columbia, SC: University of South Carolina Press, 2003.

Brady, Claire-Hayes. "The Book, the Broom and the Ladder: Philosophical Groundings in the Work of David Foster Wallace." In Hering, *Consider David Foster Wallace*, 24–37.

Burn, Stephen J. "Consider David Foster Wallace (Review)." *Modernism/modernity* 18, no.2 (2011): 465–68.

———. *David Foster Wallace's "Infinite Jest": A Reader's Guide*. London: Bloomsbury, 2003.

Bustillos, Maria. "Inside David Foster Wallace's Private Self-Help Library." *The Awl*, April 5, 2011. https://www.theawl.com/2011/04/inside-david-foster-wallaces-private-self-help-library/

Carroll, Noel. "Art, Intention, and Conversation." In *Intention and Interpretation*, ed. Gary Iseminger, 97–132. Philadelphia: Temple University Press, 1992.

Cavell, Stanley. "Aesthetic Problems of Modern Philosophy." In *Must We Mean What We Say?* 73–96.

———. "The Availability of Wittgenstein's Later Philosophy." In *Must We Mean What We Say?* 44–72.

———. "The Avoidance of Love: A Reading of *King Lear*." In *Must We Mean What We Say?* 257–356.

———. *The Claim of Reason: Wittgenstein, Skepticism, Morality, and Tragedy*. New York: Oxford University Press, 1999.

———. *Conditions Handsome and Unhandsome: The Constitution of Emersonian Perfectionism*. Chicago: University of Chicago Press, 1990.

———. "*Coriolanus* and Interpretations of Politics." In *Disowning Knowledge*, 143–78.

———. "Declining Decline: Wittgenstein as a Philosopher of Culture." In *This New Yet Unapproachable America: Lectures After Emerson After Wittgenstein*, 29–76. Chicago: University of Chicago Press, 2013.

———. *Disowning Knowledge in Seven Plays of Shakespeare*. Updated ed. Cambridge: Cambridge University Press, 2003.

———. "Ending the Waiting Game: A Reading of Beckett's *Endgame*." In *Must We Mean What We Say?* 115–62.

———. "Hamlet's Burden of Proof." In *Disowning Knowledge*, 179–91.

———. *In Quest of the Ordinary.* Chicago: University of Chicago Press, 1994.

———. *Little Did I Know: Excerpts from Memory.* Stanford: Stanford University Press, 2010.

———. "A Matter of Meaning It." In *Must We Mean What We Say?* 213–73.

———. "Music Discomposed." In *Must We Mean What We Say?* 180–212.

———. *Must We Mean What We Say?* 2nd ed. Cambridge: Cambridge University Press, 2002.

———. "Othello and the Stake of the Other." In *Disowning Knowledge,* 125–42.

———. *A Pitch of Philosophy: Autobiographical Exercises.* Cambridge, MA: Harvard University Press, 1994.

Cioffi, Frank. "'An Anguish Become Thing': Narrative as Performance in David Foster Wallace's *Infinite Jest.*" *Narrative* 8, no. 2 (2000): 161–81.

Cohen, Samuel. "To Wish to Try to Sing to the Next Generation." In Cohen and Konstantinou, *The Legacy of David Foster Wallace,* 59–79.

Cohen, Samuel, and Lee Konstantinou, eds. *The Legacy of David Foster Wallace.* Iowa City: University of Iowa Press, 2012.

Coyle, Deirdre. "Men Recommend David Foster Wallace to Me." *Electric Literature,* April 17, 2017. https://electricliterature.com/men-recommend-david-foster-wallace-to-me-7889a9dc6f03.

Crary, Alice. Introduction to *The New Wittgenstein,* edited by Alice Crary and Rupert Read, 1–17. New York: Routledge, 2000.

Danto, Arthur. "Philosophy as/and/of Literature." *Proceedings and Addresses of the American Philosophical Association* 58, no. 1 (1984): 5–20.

Descartes, René. "Dedicatory Letter." In *Meditations on First Philosophy.* Edited by John Cottingham, 3–7. Cambridge: Cambridge University Press, 2017.

———. *Discourse on Method.* 1637. London: Penguin, 2003.

———. "Meditation Two: Concerning the Nature of the Human Mind: That It Is Better Known Than the Body." 1641. In *Meditations, Objections, and Replies,* edited by Roger Ariew and Donald Cress, 13–19. London: Hackett, 2006.

Diakoulakis, Christoforos. "'Quote Unquote Love . . . a Type of Scotopia': David Foster Wallace's *Brief Interviews with Hideous Men.*" In Hering, *Consider David Foster Wallace,* 147–55.

Diamond, Cora. "Realism and the Realistic Spirit." In *The Realistic Spirit: Wittgenstein, Philosophy, and the Mind.* Cambridge, MA: MIT Press, 1995.

Dreyfus, Hubert, and Sean Dorrance Kelly. "David Foster Wallace's Nihilism." In *All Things Shining: Reading the Western Classics to Find Meaning in a Secular Age,* 22–57. New York: Free Press, 2011.

Eldridge, Richard, and Bernard Rhie. "Cavell, Literary Studies, and the Human Subject." In Eldridge and Rhie, *Stanley Cavell and Literary Studies,* 1–14.

———, eds. *Stanley Cavell and Literary Studies.* London: Bloomsbury, 2011.

Emerson, Ralph Waldo. "Experience." 1844. In *The Essential Writings of Ralph*

Waldo Emerson, edited by Brooks Atkinson, 307–26. New York: Modern Library, 2000.

Emre, Merve. *Paraliterary: The Making of Bad Readers in Postwar America*. Chicago: University of Chicago Press, 2017.

Finn, Ed. "Becoming Yourself: The Afterlife of Reception." In Cohen and Konstantinou, *The Legacy of David Foster Wallace*, 151–76.

Foucault, Michel, *Discipline and Punish*. Translated by Alan Sheridan. New York: Vintage, 1995.

Franzen, Jonathan. "Farther Away." In *Farther Away: Essays*, 15–53. New York: Farrar, Straus and Giroux, 2012. Originally published as "Farther Away: Robinson Crusoe, David Foster Wallace, and the Island of Solitude," *New Yorker*, April 18, 2011.

Freud, Sigmund, and Joseph Breuer. *Studies in Hysteria*. 1895. Translated by Nicola Luckhurst. New York: Penguin, 2004.

Giles, Paul. "All Swallowed Up: David Foster Wallace and American Literature." In Cohen and Konstantinou, *The Legacy of David Foster Wallace*, 3–23.

Glaser, Gabrielle. "The Irrationality of Alcoholics Anonymous." *The Atlantic*, April 2015, www.theatlantic.com/magazine/archive/2015/04/the-irrationality-of-alcoholics-anonymous/386255.

Goerlandt, Iannis. "'That Is Not Wholly True': Notes on Annotation in David Foster Wallace's Shorter Fiction (and Non-fiction)." In Hering, *Consider David Foster Wallace*, 156–71.

Hayles, N. Katherine. "The Illusion of Autonomy and the Fact of Recursivity: Virtual Ecologies, Entertainment, and *Infinite Jest*." *New Literary History* 30, no. 3 (1999): 675–97.

Hegel, G. W. F. *Aesthetics: Lectures on Fine Art*. 1835. Translated by T. M. Knox. 2 vols. Oxford: Oxford University Press, 1998.

———. *The Logic of Hegel*. Translated by William Wallace. 2nd ed. Oxford: Clarendon Press, 1892.

Heller, Nathan. "David Foster Wallace: Why He Inspires Such Devotion in His Fans." *Slate*, April 21, 2011. https://slate.com/news-and-politics/2011/04/why-david-foster-wallace-inspires-such-devotion-in-his-fans.html.

Hering, David, ed. *Consider David Foster Wallace*. Los Angeles: Sideshow Media Group Press, 2010.

Holland, Mary K. "The Art's Heart's Purpose: Braving the Narcissistic Loop of David Foster Wallace's *Infinite Jest*." *Critique* 47, no. 3 (2006): 218–42.

Horn, Patrick. "Does Language Fail Us? Wallace's Struggle with Solipsism." In Bolger and Korb, *Gesturing Toward Reality*, 245–70.

Horwich, Paul. *Wittgenstein's Metaphilosophy*. Oxford: Oxford University Press, 2013.

Howard, Gerald. "I Know Why Bret Easton Ellis Hates David Foster Wallace." *Salon*, Sept. 7, 2012. www.salon.com/2012/09/07/i_know_why_bret_easton_ellis_hates_david_foster_wallace.

Hungerford, Amy. *Making Literature Now*. Stanford: Stanford University Press, 2016.

———. "On Not Reading DFW." In *Making Literature Now*, 141–68.

Jameson, Fredric. *Postmodernism, or, The Cultural Logic of Late Capitalism*. Durham, NC: Duke University Press, 1992.

———. "Postmodernism and Consumer Society." Whitney Museum transcript, 1982. http://art.ucsc.edu/sites/default/files/Jameson_Postmodernism_and_Consumer_Society.pdf

Joyce, James. "Letter to Lady Gregory." 1902. In *Selected Letters of James Joyce*. Edited by Richard Ellman. London: Faber and Faber, 2003.

Kakutani, Michiko. "Calling Them Misogynists Would Be Too Kind." Review of *Brief Interviews with Hideous Men*. *New York Times*, June 1, 1999. www.nytimes.com/1999/06/01/books/books-of-the-times-calling-them-misogynists-would-be-too-kind.html.

———. "A Country Dying of Laughter." Review of *Infinite Jest*. *New York Times*, Feb. 13, 1996. www.nytimes.com/1996/02/13/books/books-of-the-times-a-country-dying-of-laughter-in-1079-pages.html.

Kelly, Adam. "David Foster Wallace and the New Sincerity in American Fiction." In Hering, *Consider David Foster Wallace*, 131–47.

———. "David Foster Wallace and the Novel of Ideas." In Boswell, *David Foster Wallace*, 3–22.

———. "Dialectic of Sincerity: Lionel Trilling and David Foster Wallace." *Post45*, Oct. 17, 2014. http://post45.research.yale.edu/2014/10/dialectic-of-sincerity-lionel-trilling-and-david-foster-wallace/.

Kenny, Glenn. "Why the End of the Tour Isn't Really About My Friend David Foster Wallace." *The Guardian*, July 29, 2015.

Kierkegaard, Søren. *Either/Or: A Fragment of Life*. 1843. Translated by Alastair Hannay. New York: Penguin, 1992.

———. *Fear and Trembling and Repetition*. Translated by Howard Hong and Edna Hong. Princeton, NJ: Princeton University Press, 1983.

Kirn, Walter. "Staring Either Absently or Intently." Review of *Oblivion*, by David Foster Wallace. *New York Times*, June 27, 2004. www.nytimes.com/2004/06/27/books/staring-either-absently-or-intently.html.

Konstantinou, Lee. *Cool Characters: Irony and American Fiction*. Cambridge, MA: Harvard University Press, 2016.

———. "No Bull." In Cohen and Konstantinou, *The Legacy of David Foster Wallace*, 83–112.

———. "Wipe That Smirk off Your Face: Postironic Literature and the Politics of Character." PhD diss., Stanford University, 2009.

LeClair, Tom. "The Prodigious Fiction of Richard Powers, Richard Vollmann, and David Foster Wallace." *Critique* 38, no. 1 (1996): 12–37.

Lerner, Ben. "On Disliking Poetry." *London Review of Books*, June 18, 2015, 42–43.

Lipsky, David. *Although of Course You End Up Becoming Yourself: A Road Trip with David Foster Wallace*. New York: Broadway Books, 2010.

Luther, Connie. "David Foster Wallace: Westward with Fredric Jameson." In Hering, *Consider David Foster Wallace*, 49–61.

Lyotard, Jean-Francois. *The Postmodern Condition: A Report on Knowledge*. Minneapolis: University of Minnesota Press, 1984.

Max, D. T. *Every Love Story Is a Ghost Story*. New York: Penguin, 2012.

McGurl, Mark. "The Institution of Nothing: David Foster Wallace in the Program." *boundary 2* 41, no. 3 (2014): 27–54.

Mikkonen, Jukka. *The Cognitive Value of Philosophical Fiction*. London: Bloomsbury, 2013.

Moi, Toril. "The Adventure of Reading: Literature and Philosophy, Cavell and Beauvoir." In Eldridge and Rhie, *Stanley Cavell and Literary Studies*, 17–29.

———. "Describing My Struggle." *The Point*, Dec. 2017, https://thepointmag.com/2017/criticism/describing-my-struggle-knausgaard.

———. " 'Nothing Is Hidden': From Confusion to Clarity; or, Wittgenstein on Critique." In Anker and Felski, *Critique and Postcritique*, 31–49.

———. *Revolution of the Ordinary: Literary Studies After Wittgenstein, Austin, and Cavell*. Chicago: University of Chicago Press, 2017.

Mulhall, Stephen. "Quartet: Wallace's Wittgenstein, Moran's Amis." In *The Self and Its Shadows: A Book of Essays on Individuality as Negation in Philosophy and the Arts*, 283–320. Oxford: Oxford University Press, 2013.

Murdoch, Iris. *The Sovereignty of Good*. 1970. 2nd ed. New York: Routledge, 2001.

Nussbaum, Martha. *Love's Knowledge: Essays on Philosophy and Literature*. Oxford: Oxford University Press, 1992.

Pippin, Robert B. *Fatalism in American Film-Noir: Some Cinematic Philosophy*. Charlottesville: University of Virginia Press, 2013.

———. *Henry James and Modern Moral Life*. Cambridge: Cambridge University Press, 2000.

———. *Modernism as a Philosophical Problem: On the Dissatisfactions of European High Culture*. 2nd ed. London: Wiley-Blackwell, 1999.

———. "Negative Ethics: Adorno on the Falseness of Bourgeois Life." In *The Persistence of Subjectivity*, 98–120.

———. "On 'Becoming Who One Is' (and Failing): On Proust's Problematic Selves." In *The Persistence of Subjectivity*, 307–38.

———. *The Persistence of Subjectivity: On the Kantian Aftermath.* Cambridge: Cambridge University Press, 2005.

Quine, W. V. "Semantic Ascent." In *The Linguistic Turn*, edited by Richard Rorty, 2nd ed., 168–72. Chicago: University of Chicago Press, 1991.

Raban, Jonathan. "Divine Drudgery." *New York Review of Books*, May 12, 2011, www.nybooks.com/articles/2011/05/12/divine-drudgery.

Ramal, Randy. "Beyond Philosophy: David Foster Wallace on Literature, Wittgenstein, and the Dangers of Theorizing." In Bolger and Korb, *Gesturing Toward Reality*, 177–98.

Rhees, Rush. *Discussions of Wittgenstein.* London: Thoemmes Press, 1996.

———. "Language: A Family of Games?" In *Wittgenstein and the Possibility of Discourse*, edited by D. Z. Phillips, 116–30. Oxford: Wiley-Blackwell, 1998.

Rorty, Richard. *Contingency, Irony, and Solidarity.* Cambridge: Cambridge University Press, 1989.

Ryerson, James. "Philosophical Sweep." *Slate*, Dec. 21, 2010. www.slate.com/articles/arts/culturebox/2010/12/philosophical_sweep.html.

Saval, Nikil. *Cubed: A Secret History of the Workplace.* New York: Doubleday, 2014.

Scott, A. O. "The Panic of Influence." *New York Review of Books*, Feb. 10, 2000, www.nybooks.com/articles/2000/02/10/the-panic-of-influence.

Shakespeare, William. *Hamlet.* Edited by Ann Thompson and Neil Taylor. 3rd ed. London: Arden Shakespeare, 2006.

———. *King Lear.* Edited by R. A. Foakes. London: Arden Shakespeare, 1997.

Smith, Zadie. *Changing My Mind: Occasional Essays.* New York: Penguin, 2010.

Sullivan, John Jeremiah. "Too Much Information." *GQ*, May 2011, www.gq.com/story/david-foster-wallace-the-pale-king-john-jeremiah-sullivan.

Swartz, Aaron. "What Happens at the End of *Infinite Jest*?" *Raw Thoughts* (blog), Sept. 16, 2009. www.aaronsw.com/weblog/ijend.

Thoreau, Henry David. "Walden." 1854. In *"Walden" and Other Writings*, edited by Brooks Atkinson, 1–300. New York: Modern Library, 2000.

Turnbull, Daniel. "*This Is Water* and the Ethics of Attention: Wallace, Murdoch and Nussbaum." In Hering, *Consider David Foster Wallace*, 209–17.

Turner, Jenny. "Illuminating, Horrible, Etc." Review of *Although of Course You End up Becoming Yourself* and *Pale King*. *London Review of Books*, April 14, 2011, 27–29.

Updike, John. *Problems and Other Stories.* New York: Fawcett, 1985.

Vogler, Candace. "The Moral of the Story." In *Critical Inquiry* 34, no. 1 (2007): 5–35.

Wallace, David Foster. *Brief Interviews with Hideous Men*. London: Abacus, 2001.

———. *The Broom of the System*. New York: Avon, 1987.

———. "Certainly the End of *Something* or Other, One Would Sort of Have to Think." In *"Consider the Lobster" and Other Essays*, 51–60.

———. "Consider the Lobster." In *"Consider the Lobster" and Other Essays*, 235–54.

———. *"Consider the Lobster" and Other Essays*. New York: Back Bay, 2007.

———. "E Unibus Pluram." In *A Supposedly Fun Thing I'll Never Do Again*, 21–82.

———. *Everything and More: A Compact History of Infinity*. New York: Norton, 2010.

———. "An Expanded Interview with David Foster Wallace." By Larry McCaffery. In *Conversations with David Foster Wallace*, ed. Stephen J. Burn, 21–52. Jackson: University Press of Mississippi, 2012.

———. *Fate, Time and Language: An Essay on Free Will*. New York: Columbia University Press, 2010.

———. *Girl with Curious Hair*. New York: Norton, 1989.

———. *Infinite Jest*. 10th anniv. ed. New York: Back Bay, 2006.

———. "Joseph Frank's Dostoevsky." In *"Consider the Lobster" and Other Essays*, 255–74.

———. *Oblivion*. New York: Little, Brown, 2004.

———. *The Pale King*. New York: Back Bay, 2012.

———. "Philosophy and the Mirror of Nature." In *Oblivion*, 182–90.

———. "The Planet Trillaphon as It Stands in Relation to the Bad Thing." 1984. In *The David Foster Wallace Reader*, 5–19. New York: Little, Brown, 2014.

———. *A Supposedly Fun Thing I'll Never Do Again: Essays and Arguments*. New York: Back Bay, 1998.

———. *This Is Water: Some Thoughts, Delivered on a Significant Occasion, About Living a Compassionate Life*. New York: Little, Brown, 2009.

Waugh, Patricia. *Metafiction: The Theory and Practice of Self-Conscious Fiction*. New York: Routledge, 1984.

Williams, Bernard. *Shame and Necessity*. 1993. 2nd ed. Berkeley: University of California Press, 2008.

Wittgenstein, Ludwig. *Culture and Value*. Chicago: University of Chicago Press, 1984.

———. *Philosophical Investigations*. 1953. Translated by G. E. M. Anscombe. 3rd ed. Upper Saddle River, NJ: Prentice Hall, 1973.

———. *Tractatus Logico-Philosophicus*. 1921. Denver, CO: Dover, 1998.

Wood, James. "Human, All Too Inhuman." *New Republic*, July 24, 2000. https://newrepublic.com/article/61361/human-inhuman.

Woolf, Virginia. "Modern Fiction." 1925. In *The Common Reader*, 146–55. Wilmington, MA: Mariner, 2002.

Index

AA. *See* Alcoholics Anonymous

abstract reasoning, 18, 26, 30, 38, 90, 115, 125

addiction, 21, 45, 67, 69, 152n41, 152n42; indulgence in, 70; in *Infinite Jest*, 42, 59, 62, 64, 65; introspection as, 117; and self-ishness, 155n17; of Wallace, 19, 20, 61, 119

adolescence, 79, 126, 128, 129, 130; forms of rebellion learned in, 125; and narcissism, 119, 122; and passion for isolation, 92; worth as philosophical subject, 131

affect theory, 144n19

agency, 30, 31, 32, 46, 56, 108

agenda of the consciousness, 102, 103, 104, 154n15

Alcoholics Anonymous, 41, 45, 75, 125, 129; authority of, 73; and belief, 62, 63, 67; Commitments of, 69, 76; and common sense, 68; critical responses to, 61; goal of, 64; and habits of thought, 95; instructs addicts to avoid asking why, 143n18; as methodologically philosophical, 79;

picture of thinking of, 74; and reason, 65; role of in *Infinite Jest*, 66; stance on communication of, 69–70, 71; as unscientific, 150n14; and Wittgensteinian challenge, 13

Ambassadors, The (James), 30–31, 32

America (United States) and Americans, 42, 66, 67, 124, 128, 131

American Dream (Mailer), 154n7

Anscombe, G. E. M., 26, 27, 28, 31

anxiety, 32, 48, 53, 70, 75; abstract reasoning leads to, 79; of Don Gately, 77; philosophical dimension of, 49

approach to literature, 25, 29, 37, 147n14, 148n28

Aristotle, 2

art and the arts, 10, 33, 35, 90, 128, 144n19; challenged by ancient philosophers, 1–2, 3; chief challenges of, 104; deconstructionists see as ideological, 148n33; as form of playing, 73; Hegel on, 29, 31, 85; in *Infinite Jest*, 70,

SQUARE ONE
First Order Questions in the Humanities

Series Editor: **PAUL A. KOTTMAN**

Square One steps back to reclaim the authority of humanistic inquiry for a broad, educated readership by tackling questions of common concern, regardless of discipline. What do we value and why? What should be believed? What ought to be done? How can we account for human ways of living, or shed light on their failures and breakdowns? Why should we care about particular artworks or practices?

Pushing beyond the trends that have come to characterize much academic writing in the humanities—increasingly narrow specialization, on the one hand, and interdisciplinary "crossings" on the other—Square One cuts across and through fields, to show the overarching relevance and distinctiveness of the humanities as the study of human meaning and value. Series books are therefore meant to be accessible and compelling. Rather than address only a particular academic group of experts, books in the Square One focus on what texts, artworks, performances, cultural practices and products mean, as well as how they mean, and how that meaning is to be evaluated.

———

PAULA BLANK
Shakesplish: How We Read Shakespeare's Language

PAUL A. KOTTMAN
Love As Human Freedom

ADRIANA CAVARERO
Inclinations: A Critique of Rectitude